THE ULTIMATE CHURCH

AN IRREVERENT LOOK AT CHURCH GROWTH, MEGACHURCHES, & ECCLESIASTICAL "SHOW-BIZ"

TOM RAABE

ZondervanPublishingHouse
Academic and Professional Books
Grand Rapids, Michigan

A Division of HarperCollins*Publishers*

Requests for information should be addressed to:
Zondervan Publishing House
Academic and Professional Books
1415 Lake Drive S.E.
Grand Rapids, Michigan 49506

Library of Congress Cataloging-in-Publication Data

Raabe, Tom
    The ultimate church : an irreverent look at church growth,
megachurches, and ecclesiastical show-biz / Tom Raabe.
      p. cm.
    ISBN 0-310-54191-3
    1. Church growth. 2. Church growth—Humor. 3. Big churches—
Humor. 4. American wit and humor. I. Title.
    BV652.25.R33   1991   91-24609
    254'.5–dc20   CIP

Cover design by Church Art Works
Cover illustration by Steve Hunt
Interior design by James E. Ruark
Edited by Gerard Terpstra

Printed in the United States of America

91 92 93 94 95 96 / CH / 10 9 8 7 6 5 4 3 2 1

To the memory of a man who knew how to laugh,
Martin Luther,
history's greatest Lutheran,

and

to my dad and mom,
Bernard and Evelyn,
who have to be up there in the top million or so.

Contents

Introduction

—That's a good book.

—Which one? This one?

—Right. The one you picked off the shelf. *The Ultimate Church.*

—What's it about?

—Church growth.

—Oh, great. Just what I need—another book on church growth. I've only got 257 of these things lying around my house.

—But this one's different.

—That's what they all say.

—But this one really is.

—How so?

—It's funny.

—A lot of them are funny.

—But this one's supposed to be funny.

—I'll be the judge of that.

—Well, why don't you be the judge of that in the comfort of your own home. It's not expensive.

—Because, as I said, I need another church growth book like I need to be named "theologian of the year" by the *Wittenburg Door.*

—But this one will open your eyes to the excesses of the church growth movement.

—It's critical of church growth, is it?

—Largely so.

—Well, if it's just a diatribe, I think I'll just put this little book back on the . . .

—Wait! It's not!

—But you just said . . .

—I said it was *largely* critical. One piece is strongly pro-church growth.

—One piece?

—That's right.

—All the rest are largely critical?

—Yes.

—So, you're banking on my ability to laugh at myself to appreciate this book. To receive it in a correct spirit, see the movement's failings, and chuckle at your jokes and maybe amend my ways, eh?

—No. I'm banking on your ability to laugh at somebody you know who is just like you.

—Very funny.

—Thank you.

—I hope that's not indicative of the level of humor in this book.

—Oh no, the humor in this book is much less sophisticated.

—But, look, church growth is like a lot of things. It's both good and bad. It does raise some valid points that can benefit all.

—You're right about that. The emphasis on evangelism and outreach that church growth champions is tremendous. Also, the way it comes down on the exclusivistic, closed-circle kind of churches that aren't open to newcomers—that's a sorely needed corrective in the church today. I mean, it's not as if I'm against churches growing or anything like that. I'm an orthodox Christian who believes in the Great Commission just as they do.

—You simply don't go into that aspect of it too much, eh?

—It doesn't lend itself to my metier.

—Speaking of metier, what's the deal with these dashes you use to set off dialogue? I find it rather pretentious.

—Pretentious? *Mich?*

—Who do you think you are? James Joyce?

—It's all a part of my quest to be clever, to set this off from the average church growth book. I use all sorts of devices. Television scripts. Timelines. Q-and-As.

—Anything to rip the movement, huh?

—Not exactly. I present an alternative as well. I feel that amid all the glitz and glamor and emphasis on change at all costs there is something precious being threatened.

—What's that?

—Orthodox historic Christianity. By focusing totally on getting numbers and meeting needs, church growth overlooks the thing that really builds the body of Christ, and that is the historic faith, the confession that has united Christians for the past nineteen or so centuries and includes liturgy, creeds, and the sacraments. I don't think we can afford the accommodationistic tendencies of a movement that relies more on what works than on what is true. Anything that canonizes applied science to a point where true theology becomes a fungible commodity and is subsumed in a body of principles and practical techniques is very suspect in my humble opinion.

—Who made you an authority on this stuff?

—Oh, I don't consider myself an authority. I consider myself a martyr.

—Why? Did Zondervan include your home phone number in here somewhere?

—No. Because I read about thirty or forty church growth books to write this thing, and I've sat through more visitor-recognition segments than I care to remember.

—Oh, you are a persecuted one now, aren't you?

—And, while I'm at it, permit me to acknowledge all of the wonderful people who played such a large role in assisting me with the writing of . . .

—Oh, don't tell me. You're going to use this fabricated dialogue as a vehicle to get your acknowledgments in, too?

—Sure. Why not? Maybe somebody will actually read them this way.

—Okay, I'll humor you. Whom do you want to acknowledge?

—Well, Mike Smith, my editor at Zondervan, played a large role with his insightful direction and helpful comments. As did two other editors at Zondervan, Len Goss, who encouraged me to try this idea out with them, and Jim Ruark, who offered me much valuable advice. A friend of mine, Marianne Ownbey, helped me refine my down-home style for one of the articles in the book. Various professors at Concordia Seminary in St. Louis—Norman Nagel, Andrew Bartelt, James Voelz, Jacob Preus III, and Charles Arand—offered me their cogent thoughts, as did Christopher Mitchell. And then there's my brother, Paul, a very good theologian for whom I will be forever grateful, not only because of his theological acumen but also because he laughed at my jokes.

—And then, no doubt, there is your ever-loyal wife, who took so much care with the typing of your manuscript, etc., etc. Don't forget her.

—No way. I typed it myself. I'm not married.

—Why doesn't that surprise me?

—Now don't get personal.

—Well, I've had enough of this silliness. I believe I'll just mosey over to the self-help section and get on with my life.

—So, are you going to buy the book?

The Ultimate Church

Remember the superchurch movement of the eighties, when megachurches were in genesis and the glorification of largeness ran rampant through the Christian world? Remember how church growth pastors the world over set seemingly preposterous membership goals?

How remote it all seems in the year 2005, now that last century's novas of growth have been eclipsed by a Southern California supernova, an empire builder who twenty-three years ago brought into existence a huge amorphous web of ecclesial polity, the logical consummation of superchurch thinking. He dubbed it the "ultrachurch": First Ultra-Church of Southern California, to be precise. I am speaking, of course, of the Rev. Dr. Roy "Solomon in a Leisure Suit" Dude.

Forget Korea, Taiwan, and Brazil; disregard Lynchburg, Hammond, and Garden Grove. First Ultra of Southern California makes the Crystal Cathedral look like a house church. It lays claim to 2.5 million souls. It adds about 10,000 new members to its rolls every month, 333 per day, 13.9 per hour, and one every 5 minutes. Dude has 166, 279 cell groups, 172,346 deacons, and 12,820 full-time staff (9,543 of which are ordained clergy). The numbers are beyond comprehension: average Sunday worship attendance is 552,364, a figure amassed in 11 services averaging over 50,000 each. Worship is enhanced by 431 choirs, 25 orchestral groups, 30 children's choirs, and 16 handbell choirs. Festival-day processions look like the Rose Parade. Dude's yearly "backdoor loss" is the size of a small denomination.

I—along with twenty-nine of my fellows—sat reeling in this vertiginous onslaught of numbers, thrown at us courtesy of a video-cassette detailing the history and goals of First Ultra. In fact, each of us had a video in hand as part of the opulent "visitor recognition package" presented to each first-time visitor. (The climax of the proceedings comes at the end of each Sunday service when one tag is drawn from a hopper of visitor name tags and a new car is given to that visitor.)

We sat in the Love Room, clad in black slickers with three-inch-high letters spelling "LOVE" on the back and awaiting our guide for the 9:00 A.M. Love Tour.

Along with the grounds and facilities, it was the tour guide I wanted to see. Being an ex-usher myself, I took considerable interest in Head Usher Simon Glibface, the brains behind the revolutionary visitor-recognition program at First Ultra. The man had grown to legendary stature in conservative Christianity. Indeed, when is the last time you've seen an usher featured on the cover of *Christianity Today?* ("The Sensation with the Carnation: The Ultimate Usher for the Ultimate Church," March 16, 1998.) With his subsequent usher textbooks, autobiography (*There Is Life Beyond Name Tags,* Dude-Books, 2001), magazine (*Badge and Bulletin,* the only ushering magazine including a centerfold portrait), world-renowned "Power Greeting Seminars," and cultlike following, Glibface had almost singlehandedly brought ushering into the sunlight of ecclesiastical celebrity. To his fame are credited such innovative strategies as parking valets, tour guides, computerized seating readouts for latecomers, and Roy Dude University's School of Usherology. The man revolutionized the field. It was his brainstorm to coordinate the corps by color-coded tuxedos: sky blue for the parking valets, lime green for the greeters, and bumblebee yellow for the transportation corps. To keep his finger on the pulse at First Ultra, Glibface traditionally gave the 9:00 A.M. Love Tour.

When he stepped through the door at the conclusion of the video at promptly 8:58 A.M., a shiver swept the room. It is one of the sensations one recognizes immediately at megachurches, one of the permutations of the secular manifested onto the religious—a nimbus of celebrity that hangs above those in power. Were Dude himself to stride through the door, the hushing would be augmented exponentially. Dude has taken the role of superchurch preacher to its logical end. Nobody expects a man like Dude to be pastoral. Nobody expects him to counsel or remember names or recall faces. If Dude spent ten minutes with each of his parishioners, the task would consume his every minute—waking and sleeping—for more than forty-nine years. No, when church growth overwhelmed the evangelical market back in the 1980s, the superchurch became the goal, the prize to be won. Seminary students no longer wanted to shepherd—they wanted to ranch. And men like Dude transcended even the status of rancher; they became kings.

Glibface asked if we wouldn't mind walking. Although eight other tours, staggered two minutes apart from 9:02 to 9:16 A.M., would ride in thirty-seat electric carts and listen to guides through personal headsets, it had been a Glibface tradition since the inception of the Love Tour to take his group on foot. In a throwback to a simpler day, he spoke with no amplification.

The man was smooth. When I first learned of the color-coding system at First Ultra, I thought it the tawdriest thing to hit the church at large since colored clerical collars. But then I had not seen Glibface. The ninety-dollar razor haircut, the surgically improved visage, the tan—the man oozed California; he was golden tongued and yet not totally yielding to swarm. He played, still, off the perception that this was a church, not the Vegas strip. Let the church take from the commercial world all it will—marketing techniques, parking philosophy—but let it call itself a church. And the color-coding taken as part of the package fit. It worked.

We strolled onto the gangway, high above the 52,000-seat sanctuary. Through glass windows we could view, seven stories below, the foyer on our right, and on the left, the sanctuary, filling rapidly to capacity. Upbeat, rhythmic music filled the sanctuary as two

4,000-member choirs, one clad in fire-engine red robes, the other in silver, swayed in chorus to words flashed on two of five sixty-foot Jumb-o-Tron screens. The songleader—a mere ant with waving arms from where we stood—loomed larger than life on three other screens. Everybody sang. High-speed ramps whisked latecomers to their seats. Dude would "appear" later, Glibface said. Dude preached forty-six Sundays a year, or at least a three-dimensional forty-foot-by-twenty-foot laser image of Dude's head did. Dude himself never showed.

First Ultra had subscribed to the multicongregational super-church model, Glibface explained, offering distinctive worship experiences catering to differing tastes. Thus six services were in the Reformed tradition—three informal, three traditional—four services were charismatic, and as a sop to the creedal, confessional, liturgical, sacramental types—I was one of those—they offered "the 9:00 P.M. hour."

"Communion must take days," I marveled, envisioning 52,000 people marching down for the common cup. "Not quite," Glibface returned. "We found that communion cut into our attendance by as much as 40,000, and the services still ran well into the wee hours. Once we sang an entire hymnal, one verse of each, during the distribution. Of course, that was before Dr. Dude decided on the auxiliary stations." Glibface swept his arm over the perimeter of the sanctuary. "Forty-foot doors open and complete chancels slide forward with ministers and everything all set up. There are eighteen of those. Of course the speed ramps help. Nobody walks. A person can get from the back row to the altar in 23.7 seconds. But, now . . ." he bade us move on as thirty people clad in black "JOY" slickers entered the gangway.

"What about baptisms?" a woman asked as our faces were pulled back from the G-force exerted against them on the high-speed escalator that whooshed us to main level. "We do those in late spring," Glibface said. "We used to simply haul everybody over to Playa del Ray or El Segundo and do it in the ocean, but the city fathers squawked about extra lifeguards and whatnot; plus 10,000 to 20,000 people in white robes invading the beach area freaked out the surfers, so we decided to keep to our hundred-meter, fully land-scaped reflecting pool behind the altar." He looked specifically at me. "For the sacramental hour, twelve fonts pop up hydraulically on the sides of the chancel."

He led us into the "Cry Room." Rows and rows of cribs stretched toward the horizon. "Three-thousand-crib capacity, with one-way windows and acoustically perfect sound," Glibface was saying as we watched thousands of mothers seated beside their babies and listening to the service through headsets. "We have on hand 16,000 rattles, 4,000 dolls, 2,000 washettes, and 4,000 crib mobiles. That facility there"—he pointed toward a monstrous bin— "has the capacity to process 50,000 diapers a day."

Now the largest church in the world, a religious colossus to dwarf even that of the mighty Cho—guru to millions in the Korean revival of the eighties and nineties—First Ultra-Church of Southern California is the quintessential church growth success story.

Dispatched from seminary fresh-faced and spitting into his hands, a fighting-the-forces-of-smallness dynamo, Roy Dude arrived in 1982 with the charge of starting a mission in the beach community adjacent to Los Angeles International Airport. In a move that made his peers look like disciples of negativism, Dude immediately named his yet-to-be-established congregation the First Ultra-Church of Southern California. He billed himself as the greatest possibility thinker since Elijah, the greatest builder since Solomon. He conducted weekly television services from a rented recording studio. (Schuller at least had preached to people in cars.) Dude preached to no one, yet his technological mastery was so facile that, via adept video splicing and sound effects, his broadcast presented an eerie verisimilitude of the real thing, an eeriness that carries over to this day.

Only after he had received the first 1,000 phone calls—then and only then—did he conduct an actual, live worship service before actual, live worshipers. No tedious pounding on doors and inviting people to church, no struggling through tough days in elementary school media centers, no hand-to-mouth existence. None of that for Roy Dude. He started big and kept getting bigger.

By 1991 Dude had constructed a 10,000-seat sanctuary and set his sights on outdrawing the Los Angeles Dodgers—a goal realized the next year, a year when the Dodgers went to the World Series. In 1995 he purchased the Los Angeles International Airport when LAX moved to its current home on a landfill five miles off the coast (downwind from the 2,000-foot smog fans). One year later, faith projections were seeing reality in the present 52,000-seat sanctuary known colloquially as "the Dudedome."

Glibface had opportunity to gloss the high points in the First Ultra story as we left the cry room and gathered about him in the middle of an enormous cavern that, once worship was over, would be instantly transformed into the coffee and fellowship area with—I had to ask—8,000 coffee urns. We turned a corner in the enormous foyer and saw a huge sign that read "To the trains" with an arrow pointing to the right, another reading "To the sanctuary" pointed left. Interior directional signs. Amazing! What a testimony to basic church growth principles!

Once we were aboard, Glibface told the story of the trains, a tale he termed "one of the greatest triumphs over the forces of negativism in the history of the Christian church." It dealt with the single most inviolable principle in all of church growth: All is negotiable save one thing—parking. Once the lots are 80 percent full, it's time for expansion.

"For five years we ringed the sanctuary with lots," Glibface said. "And when those were filled, we paved lots behind them, and more behind them. Finally, in 2001, attendance plateaued at 1.8 million. And curiously, our lots were only at 71 percent capacity. It was a crisis time for First Ultra. Dr. Dude prayed and fasted for a week on Mount Baldy, and when he came down, he imparted to us the Principle of Distance Strangulation: People will not willingly walk more than three-quarters of a mile from parking spot to sanctuary. At a ballgame, maybe. At church, no way. We had near-empty lots sitting a mile from church. Obviously some type of surface transportation was needed. Dr. Dude toyed with purchasing surplus army helicopters—they seat fifty-five. But finally he chose light rail. We experienced a little backdoor loss from that—200,000 members. But we gained that number back in no time."

The train had come to rest in front of a building. I could see the sign "Faith Tower." I craned my neck for a look up. Faith Tower, one of four forty-story monoliths—the others were Prosperity, Success, and Hezekiah towers—stood at the eastern terminus of the rail system; it was testimony to Dude's emphasis on education and cell groups. He had 13,794 Sunday school classes spread through the four towers in classes ranging from five students to six thousand, with an average ratio of one teacher to twenty students.

We stepped through the sparkling unloading station—Christian Muzak urging us on—and into the lobby of Faith Tower, where phalanxes of red-clad adjutants lined the walls awaiting the opportunity to assist. Coffee urns ringed the foyer. Bibles were stacked—seemingly in unlimited supply—for those who failed to bring their own. A huge, four-sided electronic sign stood in the middle listing the myriad classes scheduled, their location, whether seating was available, and where the vacant seats were located according to a digitized floor plan. We peeked into Room 1A, a 6,000-seat auditorium on the first floor, before filing out of the tower's south entrance onto a lush grassy area the size of a football field. The area was strewn with benches and tables, the ubiquitous fountains, waterfalls, ornamental lakes, statuary, and reflecting pools. Rising prominently at the east end of this plain was some exemplary topiary—bushes fashioned into thirty-foot figures of the apostles (a sort of shrubbery version of St. Peter's in Rome). It was impressive, all right, but the evergreen sculpture between the next two buildings was the one I wanted to see.

We zipped in and out of Prosperity, and there it was. I stopped and gaped. Others reached for their 110s. Some at the fringes of our group gasped and fell to their knees. Even Glibface, who had seen it thousands of times, allowed a mirific glint to pierce his otherwise unctuous visage. Spreading here before us was a wall of shrubbery, some one hundred feet high, and into that wall had been carved four heads, three of which bore full facial characteristics, the other standing blank. This was what I had heard so much about—Mount Growthmore.

"Doctors McGavran, Wagner, and Arn," Glibface intoned in empyreal reverence. "Need I ask who the fourth head is reserved for?" I said playfully, a remark Glibface deflected with a wan smile. "Cho?" I taunted. "Schaller?" But we were off.

A breezy stroll through the printing plant revealed two huge presses in full operation, printing next Sunday's bulletin. Then Glibface took us into what appeared at first sight to be the NASA Control Center. A huge, darkened room spread below us, with banks and banks of television monitors, an attendant at each, all concentrically arranged around a gigantic, illuminated map of Los Angeles. We walked along a gangway as Glibface talked. This was the "War Room." Demographic data had been plotted on the central map with saturation areas denoted by one color, and blinking lights all around the L.A. area by others—each light representing 10,000 members. On the computer screens, workers were pulling up neighborhood profiles, cell-group configurations, Bible-class listings.

"Taking attendance must be a chore," I said, again thinking of logistics. Glibface plunged into the details. Two main-frames and 1,500 people working around-the-clock from early Monday through mid-Wednesday every week were necessary to take attendance—church, Bible class, and cell group. Anyone missing three consecutive times receives a note in the mail. Miss a fourth, and a deacon is at the door. It made perfect sense. When numbers are your *raison d'être*, you must pay the price to get those numbers. Knowing that you reach millions is hardly enough. Cold numbers are the key.

But we were running late. The 9:00 A.M. service would be dismissed in mere minutes. *That* was something I, in my logistical caprice, longed to see. Fifty-two thousand parishioners coming out of church, and 52,000 different ones going in. I expected to witness something akin to the last five minutes of Pompeii. Lucky this was not the Midwest in winter, with 52,000 pairs of boots and rubbers thrown into the mix.

While speeding through a tunnel of luxuriant palms on our way back to Sanctuary Station, I decided to pop the million-dollar question: "What of community?" I asked. "Does anybody know anybody else?" Surely this was the apotheosis of numbers for numbers' sake—the fulfillment of prophetic voices from the mainline of the 1980s.

Glibface had heard the plaint many times over. His eyes sparked as he leveled me in his sights and proceeded to offer the well-worn sixty-member argument. In any congregation of any size the maximum number in a friendship circle is sixty, he said. There are sixty you know by name, sixty you visit, sixty who constitute your group. All others are strangers, or close to it. "In the multicongregational structure," he explained, "the Bible class serves as the fellowship format. The people you know and love gather there."

"But then First Ultra is not one church, but many little churches," I said. "To claim the grandiose numbers is playing the ultimate numbers game."

"Oh, we do have congregational events," Glibface returned. "Last year's church picnic was spectacular. We caravaned out to the high desert. One hundred thousand cars on Interstate 15. The entire fleet of Sunday school buses (1,582 of them with fifty-four seats each). We had Christian singers, Christian entertainment acts. The biggest church picnic ever. Four hundred seventy tons of potato salad on hand. Two hundred thousand gallons of grape soda, 67,000 father-son softball games, 55,000 coed volleyball games, 3 million water balloons . . ."

I waved my arms in surrender, hoping to stanch this logorrheic flow, this tour de force of numerolatry. But, alas, to no avail.

". . . and, for the first time in First Ultra history, we broke the 2 million mark in bratwursts. And, of course, the event had its spiritual side, too. Our annual exercise in proclamation evangelism was an unrivaled success. Every person had a placard with one word of the Bible on it, five feet by two feet. We proclaimed Scripture word for word all the way to Hosea 13. Almost stretched to Needles. Next year we're shooting for the entire Old Testament."

Glibface inhaled, a prolepsis of more numerological effluvium, but we had arrived at Sanctuary Station. The tour had ended. Streams of people sped past the windows of our halted car, in transit either to the sanctuary, the Sunday school complex, or the adjacent esplanade, a porticoed promenade lined with shops and stalls offering the latest in ecclesiastical amenities. One store sold Roy Dude teaching tapes, another Roy Dude preaching tapes, another Roy Dude books, another Dudedome snow globes. There was a library, a bookstore, a credit union, a barber shop, and—to accommodate the yen of the hungry First Ultra parishioner—fifty-two restaurants.

Glibface offered us a genial send-off. We handed our slickers to a janissary at the door (who subsequently rushed them to the Love Room for the 10:30 A.M. Love Tour), stepped off the train, negotiated the phalanx of greeters that had mustered for us—we were each met by a personal escort at the end of the phalanx—and were thus shunted off in whatever direction we wanted.

I wanted breakfast. I hurried toward the esplanade and Roy Dude Restaurant Row. I would miss the service, yes, but—well, there's a Sunday every week. Besides, where else can you get immediate seating at 10:00 A.M. on a Sunday?

Church Growth

The Worship Experience

From Pachelbel to Clarabell: Highlights of Church Growth Worship

1720   The Rev. DuWayne "Plenty of Seats Up Front, Folks" Pachelbel fires cannon from atop his Southern California church to invite villagers to worship. Spanish galleon, sailing near shoreline, fires salvo in return, sending local inhabitants scurrying to church for protection. As villagers sprint into sanctuary, church growth committee member seated in front pew rises to shriek, "It works! It works!" Church growth worship born.

1727   Seeking to stem massive backdoor loss to local Pietistic congregation, German pastor Heinrich Schmerz distributes first worship questionnaire. Among questions: Four-hour worship services are (1) a little long, (2) definitely too long, (3) way too long. Worship services are (1) a little boring, (2) very boring, (3) *"Snarchenstadt"* (snore city).

1728   Schmerz, upon evaluating worship questionnaires, announces, *"Wir mussen Gottesdienst Spass machen"* (We must make worship fun). Idea of celebration takes hold.

1730   In attempt to "remove all popish remnants," New England church leaders republish "A Brief Discourse Against the Outside Apparel and Ministering Garments of the Popish Church."

1744   Research shows that people pray better with eyes closed, thus prompting leaders to abolish "Lord's Prayer" and other set forms as "sinful." Free prayer becomes norm.

1770   New England parishioner, tired of sitting on hard pew for two-hour sermons, brings personal seat cushion to church. Although ending in tragedy for parishioner—he is tried for witchcraft and drowned—the idea takes hold and leads to invention of not only pew pads but also air conditioning and off-street parking.

1800   Quest for novel worship experiences is written in creedal form and adopted by Philadelphia megachurch.

1804   Sartorially liberated preachers show off new threads in many sanctuaries around country.

1811   After seven consecutive days in field with no surcease for personal hygiene, Homer M. Hosehead attends church for first time. Transfixed by flying vermin hovering about his unbathed person, Hosehead begins killing flies by striking hands together. At first separated by long pauses, Hosehead's actions become more regular as he "gets the hang of it." Thus is marked first recorded instance of parishioners clapping in church.

1821   First joke employed in sermon—"There was a Congregationalist, a Baptist, and a papist swine who died, and when they arrived at the pearly gates . . ."—by New England preacher. People who do not laugh are tried for witchcraft and drowned.

1830   Worship space declericized as first lay-led worship service is conducted.

1834   Thinking preacher is wrapping up two-hour sermon at Kentucky campmeeting, Homer M. Hosehead, attending church for second time in life, shouts, "Amen." Preacher, taking it as a sign of approbation, continues preaching, prompting others to join in cry. "Amen Corner" invented.

1842   American religious leaders, troubled by clergy's showy Sunday garb, publish "A Brief Treatise on the Establishment of Business Suits as Appropriate Clerical Attire."

1847   Homer M. Hosehead attends church for third time in life wearing same clothes (unwashed) as first two times. At strategic point in service, he throws arms in air as shirt is extremely scratchy. People nearby faint in effusion of fumes. Thus worship staples—lifting holy hands and being slain in Spirit—are invented.

1880   Dictum handed down to American pastors: "All prayers to begin with words 'We just thank and praise you, Father. . . .'"

1910   Longest singing of hymn of invitation on record occurs as Pastor Jim Bob Jerry, needing one more convert to lay claim to title "Fastest Growing Church in Cowcumber County," leads congregation in singing "Just As I Am" for three solid hours in attempt to draw only known heathen in building down the aisle. Finally, at 1:30 P.M. heathen treads forward under threat of physical harm, as remainder of congregation wants to get home to see second half of Cowboys game (they were playing on the East Coast).

1934   Worship space desacralized as local basketball team, claiming, "We're just using our talents to worship God," plays three-on-three pickup game in chancel during worship service at Philadelphia church. After one "celebrant" pulls groin going over the altar for a 360-tomahawk slam, church leaders convene and invent all-purpose, utilitarian church architectural style.

1950   In attempt to lure noncommitted members from rival church, Pastor Binky Hoffman hang-glides from balcony to pulpit to deliver sermon at large suburban Chicago church.

1951   Head Deacon Johnny Joe Ed bursts through back doors of Cowcumber County church in "Creature from the Black Lagoon" suit just as invitation hymn begins.

1952   Pastor of rival Chicago megachurch, Arnie Agamemnon, commissions parachute team—their chutes bearing apposite biblical quotations—to drop into parking lot at open-air service. Gains forty new members.

1961   Pastor Binky, engaging in evangelistic one-upmanship, calls for parachute team to free-fall into baptismal pool during worship service, but winds are bad and team bursts through chancel window of rival Pastor Arnie's church, landing in ferns behind platform, whereupon they are received into membership.

1980 Crystal Cathedral aqua exudation engineer Jacques "You Play It, We Spray It" Eau overcompensates for low water pressure at California church. Parishioners in aisle seats get soaked as mid-nave fountains go berserk during opening hymn.

1982 Denver pastor dramatically places four Bronco tickets for afternoon game on table in front of sanctuary just prior to beginning of invitation hymn.

1984 Worship space dehumanized as militant animal-rights activists insist on marking the St. Francis of Assisi Day "Blessing of the Animals" by bringing "companion animals" into church, thus making worship more meaningful for all God's creatures. One toy terrier, Rex, astounds all by barking contralto descant to Handel's "All We Like Sheep."

1988 Trends in clown ministry reach apogee as the Rev. Clarabell Barclay, in costume of namesake, answers congregational questions—one honk, yes; two honks, no—during audience-participation sermon at Los Angeles megachurch.

The Ultimate Church

Making Repentance Fun

It's finally happening. After all those years of dreary, vapid, monotonous church services, at long last we're finally putting some life into our worship.

No longer are we slaves to a prescribed liturgy week in and week out, but now worship is celebration, a gala event replete with chancel drama, liturgical dance, dialogue sermons, and anything that's new, exciting, meaningful, and relevant. Neither are we bound to a traditional hymnal anymore, as guitars and synthesizers offer commonplace accompaniment to contemporary praise music. *Everybody* has a children's sermon these days. The passing of the Peace is *de rigueur* in most churches, with the more liberated ones opting for a kiss of Peace in its stead. Worshipers feel no compunction whatever against whooping it up when the spirit (small *s*) moves them during a service. People clap in church as if they were at a ballgame. Pastors deliver multimedia homilies; they roam the sanctuary as they preach; they offer monologue sermons, discussion sermons, audience-participation sermons. And parishioners dance in the aisles, break into small groups, and voice their liberation from the pews.

Yes, it took a couple hundred years, but finally the scales have fallen from our eyes, and we can see that the conclaves in the big rooms with the funny benches and funny windows that we go to every Sunday are not atrabilious exercises in somber redundancy anymore. They are alive happenings now, "with it" celebrations where anything goes. Worship these days has finally come around to being what worship always should have been—fun!

However, there remains one area of worship where the shackles of tradition have yet to be unloosed—one integral part of the service still untouched by the revolution.

I speak of repentance—the confession of sins.

Oh, those indefatigable, guilt-inducing words—how ponderously they lay on our lips: "I, a poor, miserable sinner, confess . . . all my sins and iniquities . . . offended Thee . . . justly deserve temporal and eternal punishment . . . heartily sorry for them . . . sincerely repent of them. . . ."

It's enough to get a guy depressed, these doleful, heavy-hearted phrases, underscoring all sorts of sordid, unpopular, theological concepts.

And the people, quite understandably, are not enamored with this type of material. Consider the ordeal we subject them to, dragging out their dirty souls for inventory every week and finding—without fail—that they do not meet the supernal requirements. All that groveling, all that mental and emotional prostration—let's face facts, people do not get into that scene. No wonder they aren't coming to church.

It's a pity we can't simply write the whole business out of the service—just forget about it all and get on with being happy. But, alas, we *are* Christians. The Bible does have a few words to say about repentance and forgiveness, so we have to keep some of this stuff in. But nobody said we had to make it so depressing.

The solution to this problem is simple: We must make repentance fun. If our theology prescribes that we do this confession thing, we might as well make it something that people can get into.

However, changing minds in this area is difficult—so high have the walls of resistance been built. Bringing a congregation into the fresh rays of new meaning is bound to be a tough sell. But it can be done.

A variety of innovative methods can be used, including the passing of mirrors down the pews, followed by spoken confession, or the artistic rendering of individual transgressions via canvas and oils, fingerpaints, or even crayons. Such methods are far superior to the incantatory droning from pastor and people currently used in most faith communities.

However, lest the penitential environment grow too cumbrous during any of these soul-searching activities—and this incidentally represents a real concern, because we all know the kind of guilt trip repentance can lay on a person—the pastor would be well-advised to bring perspective back into the proceedings. My recommendation is to apply great quantities of happy-face stickers to the kneelers as constant reminders to worshipers that repentance is not some lugubrious hand-wringing exercise of blame, but that, *au contraire,* it is fun.

Perhaps the most effective means of rendering repentance enjoyable, however, is the role-playing sermonic drama. Here's how it works:

At a foreordained point in the sermon, the pastor, pausing to espy a forewarned parishioner reading his bulletin in an ostentatious manner, points toward the play-acting miscreant and reprimands him from the pulpit: "Byron Beanface! You're not listening to my sermon!" The congregation will likely gasp in outrage, and the inattentive parishioner raises his back in feigned anger. A parishioner from the other side of the sanctuary, again a willing player in the drama, then yells, "None of you people over there are listening. You're all lousy Christians!" to which a retort such as "Oh yeah? At least we have our eyes open during the sermon" is issued from the first side. That comment is followed by something like "We close our eyes because it helps us to listen better" from the second side, which is answered by "Then why do you have them open during the prayers?" from the first side, which in turn draws a response of "How do you know we have our eyes open during the prayers unless your eyes are open, too?" from the second side, and so on, back and forth.

The pastor, for his part, need do nothing more to stoke the fires of acrimony than lean over the front of the pulpit, point randomly at individual parishioners, and scream, "You whited sepulcher!" "You stinking hypocrite!" "You lousy, smelly sinner!" and such like, over and over again.

If handled properly, the scenario can easily escalate into a vigorous, comminatory shouting match, with participants from both sides of the sanctuary rising to their feet to castigate, en masse, those of the other side. When the anger has reached an acceptable level, the creative pastor then descends from the pulpit in the irenic splendor of a circus clown suit, into which he has furtively changed while in the pulpit, and juggles a few Bibles.

This readies the group for the Absolution. And what of this necessary part of the service? Must it also whither into obsolescence through the usual staid pronouncement of forgiveness? Not if the pastor is smart and creative.

The Absolution must be made fun, too.

Difficult though it is within the constructs of some liturgies, Absolution can be rendered in an effective and meaningful manner. One soul-releasing moment shines brightly in my memory. During a service once, the fellow sitting next to me fell victim to intense feelings of guilt. The Absolution had been pronounced, yet he sat moping in the pew, head bowed, shaking from side to side. He represented a disgusting reminder of the power of false guilt. So, at the pastor's direction, a group of parishioners descended upon him, picked him up, and to a spontaneous ovation carried him on their shoulders once around the congregation in a sort of victory lap for forgiveness, after which they deposited him in a nearby locker-room shower, turning on the water and cleansing him ritually. It was a beautiful moment. Sure, it wasn't all that much fun for the guy—he had a five-hundred-dollar suit on—but it imbued the ritual with meaning and brought home the significance of the Absolution in a very real way to the congregation as a whole.

Be it Confession or Absolution, repentance or forgiveness, when we can render these abstractions palpable and active—in short, fun—then we know that we've done our job.

Send them away happy. They *will* come back.

"Sunday Morning Worship"

(Theme song by well-known country rocker begins: "Are you ready? Are you ready? Are you ready for some worship? For a Sunday morning party? . . ." Theme song ends. Cut to shot of frontal silhouette draped in fog and fast-moving clouds.)

FRANK (*portentously*): His name is the Reverend Bevin Smarm. Out of obscurity he has risen in five quick years to claim the fastest-growing church west of the San Bernardino Mountains. He's colorful; he's innovative; he's relevant; he has twelve-thousand members; and he's coming to you this morning *live* from his Tabernacle of Glory in suburban Los Angeles. (*Clouds drift away from silhouette to reveal fully lighted face of Rev. Smarm as theme song heightens to crescendo and then stops. Cut to Frank in booth.*) Hello, everybody. Welcome to ABC's "Sunday Morning Worship." Sitting at our vantage point at mid-nave, high atop the Tabernacle of Glory, I'm joined by some very special guest commentators, brought back to celebrate this tenth anniversary special edition of "Sunday Morning Worship." Dandy Don, welcome. (*Pan to Don.*)

DON: Howdy, folks.

FRANK: Good to have you back. And the third spoke in our famous broadcasting wheel—some would say the hub . . .

HOWARD (*sententiously*): I would say the hub.

FRANK: . . . I welcome the inestimable, the bodacious, the irrefragable, the uh . . . uh . . .

HOWARD: Omniscient.

FRANK: . . . the omniscient and ever-so-humble one himself, Howard. (*Pan to Howard.*)

HOWARD: It is a singular honor—Frank, Dand-er-oo—to once again occupy a seat in this booth with such un-im-peach-a-ble talent. (*Shouting*) And what an occasion! (*Normal voice*) The Reverend Bevin Maximilian Smarm, known to his parishioners simply as Pastor Biff—the o-le-a-gi-nous one—celebrating five years in the Tabernacle of Glory pulpit today, this morning on "Sun-day Mor-ning Wor-ship."

FRANK: There's action in the sanctuary, gentlemen. (*Cut to organist, who is playing vigorously.*) It's the organ prelude. Sound familiar?

DON: It ain't "In the Garden," I can tell you that much.

HOWARD: Indeed not, Dand-er-oo. (*Shouting*) It's the "Toc-cat-ta and Fugue in D Min-or." (*Normal voice*) Jo-hann Seb-ast-i-an Bach. Majestic. Imposing. Exalted. One of the war-horses of the gen-re.

FRANK: I see a trend here, Howard. When we did the Tabernacle three years ago it was Widor's "Toccatta from Symphony No. 5." Two years ago, Mulet's "Thou Art the Rock." All rousing, energetic selections. Last year, as I recall, she simply played Camille Saint-Saens's "Three Great Chords" for five minutes.

DON: 'Course, boys. It's noisier than a pack of feminists dialoging with Jerry Falwell down there.

HOWARD: Right you are, Dand-er-oo. An un-con-scio-na-ble display of ir-rev-er-ence. The gabbing throngs. The scandalous in-form-al-i-ty of worship. (*Somberly*) It is tantamount to a symbol of megachurch worship. And taken in concert with the architectural min-i-mal-ism of the structure, all too typical of the modern meg-a-church. Archaeologists three hundred years from now will think this edifice was a business park. (*Pan the sanctuary.*)

FRANK: I see what you mean, Howard. And inside, of course, the effect is the same. The auditorium look. No altar. No paraments. No stained glass. No clerestory windows. Just a platform up front with a stand in the middle. The choir situated behind the platform for a concert-stage effect. And padded theater seats and thick wall-to-wall carpeting.

DON: The ferns behind the platform speak to my heart, guys.

FRANK (*laughing*): What do they say, Don?

HOWARD (*gravely*): Call it the Cal-i-forn-i-ca-tion of the church. The symbolism of the liturgical church rejected by latter-day iconoclasts as meaningless at best and de-mon-ic at worst. And in its place rise up the symbols of affluence, the trappings of comfort, a mon-u-ment to the eth-os of con-sum-er Am-er-i-ca.

FRANK: The congregation is standing. Looks like we're ready to go. Let's listen in.

(*Cut to congregation, all standing, which sings four verses of "To God Be the Glory," the stanzas embellished by interstanza organ interludes, the last of which is highlighted by a choral descant from the forty powder-blue-clad choristers standing behind the platform.*)

DON: That is some kind of singing.

HOWARD: Very true, Don. And it would emit an ambience of worship were it followed by traditional set forms like the Invocation, the Confession of Sins, and the Introit, the Kyrie, and the Gloria—in short, by the historic Entrance Rite of the church—wherein one is ushered into the presence of God, as it were, there to embark upon the elements of divine worship, to wit: the service of God to the sinner and the con-com-i-tant response of the sinner to God, in that order. (*Morosely*) But no, what do we have here?

(*Cut to assistant minister at podium, who gushes, "Good morning!" To which congregation responds with a tepid smattering of unenthusiastic "Good mornings." Assistant minister shouts, "Good morning!" again louder. This time the reply is thunderous. Announcements are then made, after which the assistant minister walks off stage, replaced at the podium by the Reverend Smarm and an impeccably coiffed young man— Harry Helmethead—who does the weather for a local television station. Smarm asks Helmethead a question and a dialogue ensues.*)

FRANK: The celebrity testimonial. A hallmark of the evangelical megachurch.

DON: I'll take it any day over the dry-as-a-Nazarene-bachelor-party theological spiel you get in some churches.

FRANK: It does highlight the experiential—a spoken, personal testimonial to the power of God's grace.

HOWARD: In-ter-est-ing ob-ser-va-tion, Frank. I did lunch with Pastor Biff just yesterday and brought up this very issue.

(Cut to office setting with Howard and Bevin sitting side by side on two chairs.)

HOWARD *(in hushed voice)*: Biff, the celebrity testimonial. Is it not yet another example of the an-thro-po-cent-ric nature of consumer Christ-i-an-i-ty? Yet another horizontal di-ver-ti-men-to in the divine vertical antiphonal dialogue that is rightly ordered wor-ship, the vestiges of a re-viv-al-is-tic past?

BEVIN: Uh, well, I don't know, Howard.

HOWARD: Is not the tacit message one of in-tro-spec-tive sub-ject-i-vi-ty? A validation of truth based on ex-per-i-en-tial feel-ings?

BEVIN: Uh, well . . . I guess the message is the same in all testimonials, Howard. And that is that Christianity is true because it worked for me. Because, you see, Jesus just doesn't sell, Howard. But putting people up there who can tell us what Jesus did in their lives does. And celebrity status makes it all the more powerful.

HOWARD: The resultant message being, Biff, that we should accept Jesus because Harry Helmethead does?

BEVIN: Uh, something like that.

(Cut back to Howard in the booth.)

HOWARD: Tel-ling it like it is, Frank. "It must be true if it's true for you."

DON *(singing)*: It must be troo-oo-oo, if it's true for yoo-oo-oo.

FRANK: Interesting. . . . Bringing you up to date on what transpired in the sanctuary while we were away, the service has been pushing full bore to the climactic sermon. Recapping, a lay reader delivered the Scripture lesson.

DON: Obviously, a student in the Robert Anthony Schuller School of Scripture Reading.

HOWARD: Which is to say, Dand-er-roo, that it was delivered in an a-bys-mal-ly his-tri-o-nic man-ner.

DON: He did sound like he was trying out for a high school play.

FRANK: And then there was the anthem. Forty voices raised high in a patriotic medley composed by the Tabernacle's minister of music, Myron Mott. A chandelier-shaking performance. Which was followed by a pastoral prayer, for which the congregation held hands.

HOWARD (*excitedly*): And during which the organist saw fit to lend accompaniment with that insipid, treacly mood music that is more the staple of the *Schwaermeri* than it is of state-ly wor-ship.

FRANK: And that brings us to the offertory and a highlight of every "Sunday Morning Worship" telecast, the "Offertory Highlights," a review of momentous ecclesiastical events in growing churches of a week ago. Take it away, Howard.

(Theme song begins in background as camera cuts to prerecorded highlights of various worship services of the previous week from around the country, which are shown as Howard does the voice-over.)

HOWARD: Cleveland's Antipedobaptism Nondenominational Church and its organist of world renown, Tru-dy Trem-o-lo—the sens-u-ous sweetie of the swell ped-al. (*Hushed tone*) Here seen caught in the embarrassing contretemps of choosing her postlude during the sermon. (*More excitedly*) But a few short moments later finding redemption by making that Rogers organ shake with emotion. (*Shouting*) Listen to that vi-brat-o! . . . (*Normal voice*) The scene: Dallas's Temple of Tongues. The *artiste*: Bop "I'll Do Anything to Increase Attendance" DuPre. (*Shouting*) Playing the saxophone with his toes! Look-at-him-go! . . . (*Normal voice*) And then there was the touching scene at Seattle's Angst Be Gone Lutheran Church, where lay readers Connie and Bart Torgeson made manifest the true unity of their marriage in an emotional antiphonal reading of the epistle lesson, Connie reading one verse, Bart the next. . . .

(*Excitedly*) And what of the liturgical extravaganza at Chicago's John Paul George Ringo Catholic Church! Streamers. Banners. And a Dionysian release of three thousand balloons from subfloor vaults in the sanctuary. (*Shouting*) Look-at-them-go! They could go all-the-way! (*Hushed tone*) Unfortunately, they did. All the way to the ceiling, that is, where many balloons popped as they struck the various and sundry pointed objects in the in-ter-i-or of the sanc-tu-ar-y. . . . (*Excitedly*) And who was not viscerally moved by the innovations of the neoteric Anthrax "The Puppet Man" Cole of Atlanta's Jump for Joy Episcopal Church (*hushed tone*), here seen allowing two of his most recent creations, Dolly and Slim, deliver the hom-i-ly from the pul-pit. (*Theme song crescendos, stops; cut back to sanctuary.*)

FRANK: Hello again, everybody. We trust you were edified by those offertory highlights. And now we have a treat here at the Tabernacle of Glory. A highlight of every worship service, the vocal solo number, this morning to be delivered by the tabernacle's own internationally known recording artist, Mercedes Goodpipes, who will sing her most recent hit, "Shall We Gather in the Narthex," a vocal manifesto to fellowship.

(*Mercedes, clad in hot-lime chiffon wraparound dress, begins singing.*)

FRANK (*whispering*): That's odd. Her lips aren't matching the music. Is it a lip-sync, gentlemen?

DON: Gotta be. I don't see any violins, and I hear about a couple philharmonics' worth of 'em.

HOWARD: The de-test-a-ble, ex-e-cra-ble ac-com-pa-ni-ment track, a meretricious sacralization of the vulgar that has no worthy role what-so-ev-er in the . . .

FRANK: No, Howard, I mean the words. I don't even think she's singing the words. Let's see that again.

(*Cut to replay of Goodpipes' song, in which movement of her lips trails by an infinitesimal lapse of time the booming forth of the lyrics on the tabernacle sound system.*)

FRANK: The people like it, though. Listen to that applause!

HOWARD: Clapping in church! (*Somberly*) Yet another shameless cap-it-u-la-tion to the zeit-geist, a further erosion to the concept of rev-er-ence in wor-ship.

DON: Will you look at that! Well, I'll be smothered in a woolly chasuble!

(Muffled cries of excitement from announcers as Smarm approaches the lectern for the sermon. Cut to Smarm.)

FRANK: Those of you watching this in black-and-white are really missing something here.

DON: Brother! How that tie does *shine!*

HOWARD: Resplendent in patterned neckware of ornate and meticulous workmanship, with small open Bibles set against what appears to be an incandescent color of indeterminate hue, the Rev-er-end Be-vin Max-i-mil- . . .

DON: Indeterminate hue? Tell it like it is, Howard. That's traffic-cone orange!

HOWARD (*laughing*): So it is, Dand-er-oo.

DON (*shouting*): Unbutton the jacket, Biff!

HOWARD (*somberly*): Oh, how the church could use a renaissance of the humility and anonymity embodied in the ut-il-i-za-tion of cler-i-cal robes. (*Voice rising*) Which hid the personality of the homilist. Which drew attention to his words and not his appearance. (*Shouting*) But no! (*Voice hushed*) The idea has been rejected by the evangelical powers that be, thrown onto the ash heap of symbolic ostentation along with chancel furnishings, well-ordered liturgical proceedings, and a myriad of accoutrements of fifteen centuries of ec-cles-i-as-ti-cal his-tor-y.

FRANK: The crowd is hushed. Biff is beginning the message. Let's listen in.

(Cut to lectern. The Rev. Bevin Smarm—employing his signature "a joke and an aphorism" homiletic style—delivers his homily, "How to Build Better Relationships," a prototypical evangelical message centered on applying biblical principles to daily living, in which Smarm pushes all the right buttons, offering well-defined points and practical

guidance to help his members make sense of this uncertain world. Upon completion, the organist embarks upon some mood music, heavy on the tremolo, as Smarm delivers an extempore and lengthy prayer, over which the announcers speak.)

FRANK: Pretty basic stuff, wouldn't you say, podners?

DON: It hit them right where they live, Frank. Basic how-tos. These folks are interested in making it work in their lives.

HOWARD: Indeed they are, Dand-er-oo. Lifestyle. It is quintessential evangelical Christianity—evocative of an anathema toward apologetics and the elevation of mind-set and style of personal piety to an ap-o-the-o-sis of its kind. That's what unites these people—their experiences with the lifestyle.

(Smarm wraps up his prayer and spreads his arms for the benediction.)

DON *(singing)*: Turn out the lights! The party's o-o-ver-r-r!

FRANK *(excitedly)*: Look at the choir!

HOWARD: No!

DON: Not the Gatorade!

HOWARD *(laughing)*: Director Myron Mott is going to feel a sudden change in the humidity!

(All laugh as the postlude—"Theme and Variation on 'Shall We Gather in the Narthex'"—begins. The congregation stands, chattering en masse, and begins its exodus to the foyer. Theme song starts. Cut to Frank in booth.)

FRANK: We hope you enjoyed this presentation of "Sunday Morning Worship." On behalf of all of us here at ABC—Don, Howard, me, our executive producer, and the boys in the truck—we bid you a pleasant morning.

(Theme song crescendos, stops. Fade to black.)

Passing the Peas

In much the same way as others may recall their first communions, their first Christmas pageants, or other significant "firsts" of their church lives, I remember my first passing of the Peace.

And a glorious moment it was too—exciting and exhilarating, like a wave of animation engulfing a heretofore staid, cheek-sucking congregation—for a few minutes anyhow.

I remember it well—the noise, the eruption of fellowship, the pastor getting lost. All churchly decorum as I knew it fled before the face of this spontaneous and sincerely rendered *Gemütlichkeit*. Pastors and pastoral adjutants cascaded down the chancel steps, their robes billowing as they ranged far afield, reaching for hands, tweeking biceps, winking at children. People grabbed each other's hands as well. They pummeled each other's backs and greeted each other warmly and—shock!—actually laughed out loud in church. For a few moments the congregation had unified around one objective—sharing the peace of the Lord.

Those around me made great efforts to ensure that I got my share, too. The person to my left got right up close and flashed me a smile the size of a building-fund pie chart, while the man behind me grabbed my hand as if we were engaged in some sort of pro wrestling contest, and the woman in front of me refused to let me go until I had divulged to her my complete genealogical history. The fellow to my right, despite my adamant and histrionic objections, decided it necessary to offer me a hug of Peace.

It was a wonderful moment indeed, a veritable oasis amid the wilderness of stagnating redundancy we call liturgy. And it proved to me one vital, life-changing point, one truism I will never forget: Given the right set of circumstances, even the frozen chosen can show a little life.

But, oh, how fleeting were those flights of liturgical exhilaration. Alas, with repetition the exuberance faded. Every week the ritual became a little more familiar, a little less exciting. Soon it was the same old, same old—pressing a little flesh, slapping a few backs, peering into an eyeball or two—until finally, regrettably, I found myself just going through the motions.

I found I was not the bubbling fount of sanguine good cheer I had been previously. I was not climbing across bodies to get to somebody a little distance down the pew. The fellow three pews away on the aisle whom I formerly roamed off to greet—now I was simply waving at the guy.

The wondrous event of the passing of the Peace had lost its spark, its theological significance, at least for me.

Questions began to nettle. Was I alone a mindless slave to this ritualized convention, or were others experiencing a similar ennui? Could the meaning of the ritual be saved? Could it be rescued from the black hole of liturgical irrelevance? For the sake of modernity, should we go to high-fiving the Peace?

These questions probed and nagged at me until I accidentally stumbled on an answer. What was needed was a palpable, tangible reminder of the significance of this liturgical event, something to awaken us to the Christian peace we exchange during that special moment. And what tangible object would best fill these needs?

It came to me one evening as I bent over the hot coils.

Peas.

In addition to the obvious paronomastic nexus—*peas* and *peace*—there is also a theological connection. Peas, unlike some garden vegetables, grow in community—the pod. How significant that when we pass the Peace we affirm the theological importance of community.

If this rubric has lost its meaning for you, why not bring along to church next Sunday a small baggie of frozen peas? At the appropriate time during the service, open the bag, take out individual peas and hand them to your fellow parishioners with your left hand, while shaking their right hands and greeting them with the words, "The peas of the Lord be with you," or simply, "The peas of the Lord."

I know the traditionalists among us will lapse into reflexive knee-jerk conniption fits over this suggestion. I can hear them now: "We've had the passing of the Peace for as long as I can remember, and we've never done this thing with peas before. This is a church. This ain't no grocery store."

But there are always those who don't like anything new, those who gripe about every novel, meaningful means of expression we try to incorporate into worship, people so mindlessly tied to the old ways that they are in danger of losing the true meaning behind what they're doing.

As we strive for fresh meaning through worship renewal, let us beware the rhetoric of the misoneists, those purblind ecclesiastical Luddites who employ as defense against innovation the seven last words of the church: We never did it that way before.

Instead, let us issue as rejoinder seven words that can start us on our way to liturgical relevance: When passing the Peace, pass the peas.

Oh, yeah. They found him in his study.

Church Growth

The Theological Contours

The History and Theology
of the Church Growth Movement
(Fractured Version)

Theologies, while radically diverse in emphasis and direction, almost always develop along very predictable lines. A leading thinker trots some new doctrine out into the field. His peers ruminate on its validity. Excoriating reviews are published; defenders mount a counterattack; epithets are hurled; the tenets are revised; the revision is attacked; the thinkers revise even more; and eventually, distilled over time, a unified whole emerges. There's a dynamic to it all.

After all, Luther didn't pound his Ninety-five Theses onto the Wittenberg church door and then hie off to veg out in the Côte d'Azur for the rest of his life. (The guy in the fancy hat said bull to that.) There were debates and treatises and get-back *pronunciamentoes* and wars and *auto–da–fé*s and alliances and everything else that constitutes the Reformation scene.

So it has been with the church growth movement. Since its genesis some thirty-five years ago, it has been wracked with controversy. Many have been the broadsides fired against the doctrines of church growth. And many have been the salvos of rebuttal returned from Fortress Pasadena. Principles have been attacked; church growth revisions have been effected; names have been used; words have been exchanged.

But a definitive theological treatment written in historically accepted theological terms has yet to be penned. The Lutherans have their justification by grace through faith, the three *solas*, and the law-gospel dialectic and have written, as a confessional enunciation of the same, the *Augsburg Confession* and its related *Apology*. The Calvinists have their material principle—the sovereignty of God—made plain in Calvin's *Institutes*. The Romans have their reliance on Scripture *and* church tradition, all spelled out in works such as the *Vatican Decrees*. And all have included many important phrases written in Latin and lots of high-and-mighty terms.

So what does church growth offer as a succinct theological encapsulation? It offers books with mundane titles like *Understanding Church Growth*, *How to Grow a Church*, *I Believe in Church Growth*, and *Strategies for Church Growth*. And the doctrinal issues? They sound as if they were invented by a frustrated sociologist whose idea of a wild and crazy Saturday night is rearranging his sock drawer: the homogeneous unit principle; the Resistance-Receptivity Axis; composite church membership; multi-individual, inter-dependent decision; E-2, 3-P evangelism;[1] etc.

Not to put too fine a point on it, but this stuff is B-O-R-I-N-G!! There's no panache to it, no charisma, no, well, *gravitas*. And it's all in English! Perhaps this is due to the fact that church growth is in reality not theological at all, but sociology gussied up in theological drag, and this is simply how sociology-cum-theology comes out of the word processor. Or it might emanate from a populistic desire to remain perspicuous to pastors who graduated from seminaries that soft-pedaled the classical languages and church history. Of this, only Pasadena knows for sure.

Whatever the reason, it's high time somebody sat down and wrote the thing up proper—with Latin terms and official names and footnotes[2] and all of the other trappings one comes to expect from truly scholarly prose. With the aforesaid in mind and with humble

---

1. Wasn't that the name of the little mechanical guy in *Return of the Jedi*?

2. *Lots* of footnotes.

The Ultimate Church

but risible heart, we herein offer the fractured version of the history and theology of the church growth movement.

A Historical and Theological Overview

Appropriately, the church growth movement[3] began with a survey, the now-famous Pickett's Survey,[4] which revealed that the decadal growth rate of 134 mission stations in India stood at only 12 percent. Donald A. McGavran, the universally acknowledged founding father of the movement, read the survey, was troubled by the results, and coincidental with the fortuitous self-discovery of *auctus ecclesiae oculi*,[5] sent forth a phalanx of researchers marching behind the banner of the Great (Growth) Commission: "Go ye therefore and study growing churches and find out what works."

Forth they did go, scouring the growth statistics of mission stations throughout the subcontinent, and back they did come, toting a copious body of data that was shortly thereafter codified, brought forth in printed form (the *Codex Census*),[6] and sent throughout the world. Patterns began to emerge, and doctrine was set down; the lineaments of the mass conversion, with its corollaries—the homogeneous unit principle and evangelizing the "masses not the classes"— were quickly canonized.

However, the movement still lacked theological definition; so the formal and material principles—the source of the movement's doctrines and its central theological idea, respectively—were formulated and officially decreed. These principles took the following form:

---

3. This name narrowly won out over "The Christian Society for Propagating the Gospel Among Heathen Hordes" and "The General Missionary Convention of the Various Denominations in the United States for Foreign Missions."

4. Not to be confused with Pickett's Charge.

5. "Church growth eyes."

6. This bible of the movement is revised continually and is used for the ritualistic church growth procedure of "removing the fog."

• Formal Principle: God is interested in results in evangelism, not effort or faithfulness to his Word;[7] and those results are to be made manifest in "responsible church membership."

• Material Principle: Whereas the Lutheran Reformation focused on three *solas*, the church growth movement holds but one, *solus practicus*.[8] This is the linchpin of the movement and has generated many ancillary doctrines—the theology of methodology, the Resistance-Receptivity Axis, and soil testing, to name three.

Shortly after its promulgation, the formal principle (the most concise rendering of which took the form of the Glasser Confession—"The church that does not grow is out of the will of God")[9] met heavy resistance. This health-and-wealth dictum given church growth contours drew blood to the faces of traditional ecclesiasts the world around. What of the myriad inner-city and rural parishes that remain bastions of nongrowing faithfulness? they cried. Surely they too stand well within the bounds of God's good will. Church growth heeded its critics, and the First Great Amelioration[10] was propounded. For such churches, called victims of various esoteric diseases,[11] growth was to be measured internally.

---

7. Jesus was success oriented; Acts is results oriented.

8. The Rev. Robert Schuller's *solas* (*sola parking, sola accessibility, sola visibility* et al.) are derivative and not to be taken as normative.

9. I am not making this up.[63] The quote can be found in Delos Miles, *Church Growth—A Mighty River* (Nashville: Broadman, 1981), 74.

10. Also called "Wimp-Out I," this modification of doctrine became the archetype for many more to follow. The amelioration process usually goes like this: Inevitably someone somewhere (almost always an impossibility thinker [*cogitans negationes*]) points out defects in a church growth pronouncement; the curia calls a conclave; the cardinals of growth then repair to the Holy See; and shortly thereafter the white smoke of doctrinal reformulation arises from the Pasadena chimney in the form of a new church growth book or two.

11. "Ethnikitis" and "ghost town disease" are two such terminal diseases, and along with their nonterminal fellows ("koinonitis," "hypercooperativism," etc.), are always described in terms of growth. Nongrowing churches, whether stricken terminally or not, are diseased.

The Ultimate Church

However, ameliorated or not, the formal and material principles of the theology seemed sadly misdirected to many. The cry went up from *homines religiosi* throughout the world: "That's not theology; that's sociology!" And Growthmen[12] were forced to elucidate bona fide theological principles. These came down in the form of the Non-Negotiables,[13] a modest listing of five or six fundamental conservative beliefs, which, having been officially stated, could then be shunted aside to make room for the real mission of the church. The Non-Negotiables are, in short, *assumed*, a body of afterthought never at the fore and tacked onto the sociological canon in order to quell the officious tongues of naysayers. The sociology-theology debate still rages. Some ecclesiasts question whether a movement fueled by what works and not by what is true can ever be considered truly theological.[14]

The Numerological Controversies

Just as the church was beset with many volatile and formative controversies in its early years (Arianism, Docetism, Monarchianism, Manichaeanism, the debate regarding *homoousios* versus *homoiousios*,[15] etc.), so too has the church growth movement been

---

12. This is not a sexist term as applied to church growth leaders; it is descriptive.

13. Not to be confused with the Negotiables, an amorphous body of doctrine the Growthmen consider beyond their purview. Growthmen are in reality doctrinal pluralists par excellence; doctrines are fungible commodities. Indeed, *doctrine*, in any classical understanding, is pretty much a dirty word in church growth circles; it gets in the way of growth. Pastor X adheres to the Five Fundamentals; Pastor Y goes charismatic; Pastor Z is Arminian down to the last erg of his free will. No problem. If Pastors X, Y, and Z are getting the numbers, their theologies must be okay.

14. It's one thing to maintain that God requires faithfulness to his Word and that from such faithfulness will accrue growth. It's quite another to assert that God wants the church to grow and churches that do so are being faithful to his Word. In short, if it works, it must be God's work. Critics call this a theology of glory, an anthropocentric theology with man at the levers.

15. Not to be confused with the homogeneous unit principle.

forced to evaluate one of its primary doctrines: the supremacy of numbers. One leading commentator of an earlier age encapsulated church growth's vision with the words "The bigger the better."[16] Almost immediately, the theology of the formal principle was challenged by a group calling itself the "Resistible Willers." God wants churches to grow, they agreed. It is truly God's will that more people join them. But just because God wills it, the Resistible Willers claimed, doesn't mean it must happen. In short, God's will is resistible in church growth just as it is in individual conversion—after all, God also wills that everyone be saved. To thus evaluate evangelism through success—i.e., numbers—is misleading at best, a heretical outrage at worst. This debate also continues, with Resistible Willers often opting for truth (what ought to be) rather than results (what is).

Growthmen, however, have mounted up a defense—*enumero populum* [because][17] *populus enumeratus*[18] (a shibboleth many see fit to enshrine on their church signs)—and have laid out an elaborate theological defense of their propensity to count.[19] There is nothing unspiritual about counting, they aver.

When the battle lines are drawn, critics often cite Jesus' threefold command to Peter in John 21, saying, "Jesus said to feed his sheep, not count them," and generally assuming that God uses a different sort of mathematics than mankind (the *Deus Mathematicus*).

---

16. Richie ("Big Boogers") Hanson, in personal conversation with author on relative merits of large- versus medium-sized chocolate dip cone at Carvel ice cream stand, 90th and Burleigh streets, Milwaukee, Wisconsin, July 12, 1959. (Real scholars footnote their buddies as often as possible, even when, on occasion, it doesn't have anything to do with what they're talking about.)

17. I have a cheap English-Latin dictionary.

18. "We count people because people count."

19. Jesus counted sheep, coins, grain, fish, hairs on the head, and sparrows in the air; Moses counted Israelites (so did David [1 Chron. 21:1], but that incident is not emphasized much); Luke counted converts; a book of the Old Testament bears the propitious title of Numbers.

The Ultimate Church

This emphasis has given rise to a group called the Qualitativists,[20] a dissident movement that saw its zenith in the publication of *Church Growth Is Not the Point*. This book, largely dismissed by Growthmen as just a lot of whining and justification for the mainline's declining membership, posited that, while certain denominations were indeed losing members, concomitant with that numerical loss was an increase in the quality of the remaining faithful. The Qualitativists sought to set quantity and quality in an either-or dynamic.

Growthmen everywhere rose up as one in opposition to this justification of nongrowth—after all, strip the movement of its *raison d'être* and the wheels fall off—and, in perhaps the most celebrated event of the Numerological Wars, marched en masse on Riverside Drive.[21] In neat phalanxes they paraded before the structure and sang the now-famous "Battle Hymn of the Movement" (to the tune of "Hark, the Herald Angels Sing"), the first verse of which we reprint here.

"Numbers, numbers!" is our cry,
Charts and graphs and formulae.
Stats and surveys, lots to do,
Facts and figures, growth rates too.
Special rooms for crying tots,
Bigger signs and parking lots,
We want people just like us,
Strictly homogeneous.
Hark! What do the numbers say?
Big is better, all the way.

While the crusade did prove fatal to three Growthmen,[22] it is

---

20. Also called "Remnant Theologians," the "Little Flock Party," and the "Riverside Drive Prophets" (the World Council of Churches and its domestic counterpart, the National Council of Churches, are located on Riverside Drive in New York City), these ecclesiasts subscribe to the doctrine of *gloriatio parritatis* (glorification of smallness).

21. The Numbers' Crusade.

22. They were enticed into the building, lost their way in the bureaucratic maze, and died a brutal death by starvation sometime later in a vacated mainline mission office.

best remembered for the dramatic pounding onto Riverside Drive's front door of a monumental manifesto that proved to be one of the movement's greatest successes and inflicted fatal damage to Qualitativists the world around. This was the *Qualititioque* Clause, to wit: We brook no animus toward quality. Indeed, growing churches possess quantity *and* quality.[23] Both are essential; it's a both-and situation.[24]

However, to disabuse any who might think the *Qualititioque* Clause portended a let-up on qualitative emphasis—after all, the Growthmen did back off from their numerological monomania somewhat during the First Great Amelioration—note church growth's encapsulating statement on the value of numbers. Like the famous German monk of yesteryear eyeballing the disputatious Johann Eck, church growth also claims its "Here I Stand" dictum. This has taken the form of the Wagner Profession: "The Church Growth Movement is not about to forego its use of numbers and statistics."[25]

The Mandatum Mandatorum Controversy[26]

Here we enter another fertile field of dispute—the definition of evangelism. Is it spiritual in emphasis, or temporal? Are we to preach and disciple or to help natives improve their station in life? In short, does the evangelical mandate hold sway over the cultural mandate, or vice versa?

---

23. But bear in mind that if church growth is going to impute major importance to qualitative factors, it will also deem it absolutely necessary to measure that quality. Unmeasurable abstractions are of no value to the Growthmen's Descartian dialectic of *enumero ergo sum* (I count, therefore I exist). Indeed, efforts have been made to quantify the "quality church."

24. This formula, albeit salubrious and generously accommodating on the surface, harbors the more combative and unstated subtext that threads its way through nearly all of church growth literature: Anyone who criticizes us for our numbers and growth is just a pastor of a nongrowing church who is simply jealous.

25. C. Peter Wagner, *Church Growth and the Whole Gospel: A Biblical Mandate* (San Francisco: Harper & Row, 1981), 62.

26. The "mandate of the mandates."

Originally the Growthmen came down heavily on the evangelical side—teaching the Ungabungians to rotate crops was *not* their idea of evangelism.[27] Thus, almost to the exclusion of any sort of social mandate, they emphasized making disciples in the traditional way.

However, criticism of this emphasis, being strident, forced them into reevaluation.[28] Issues like hunger, poverty, oppression, and economic and political injustice were linked inextricably to the gospel by the Culturalizers; these must be included in any proper definition of mission.

The Growthmen felt the heat. Having categorically denounced this school of mission early in the debate, they have since—influenced by the pronouncements of the Lausanne Covenant—repaired to "New Rome"[29] to effect *aggiornamento*.[30] The cultural mandate is indeed crucial and necessary, they averred. But they stopped short of placing it on equal standing with the evangelical mandate.[31]

The Great Commission Confutation

Defining the Great Commission was never a big problem in the Christian faith until the Growthmen arrived on the scene with their

27. The social action school of mission has seen evolution over the years, from "a cup of water in the name of Jesus" to "our mission to the Buddhists is to help make them be better Buddhists" to *"Viva la revolucion!"*

28. The only time church growth ever rethinks its theology, it seems, is when somebody criticizes it.

29. Pasadena.

30. Also called "The Second Great Amelioration," or in some circles, "Wimp-Out II."

31. Because, in addition to theological reasons, it doesn't work. A cultural emphasis does not grow churches. Thus the evangelistic mandate takes priority. However, the cultural mandate, as employed in a secondary role, is further dichotomized into two distinct types of social activity: social service (*ministerium profanum*) and social action (*actio profana*). The former is more individual in orientation (healings, exorcisms, etc.) and highlights the power of God so that unbelievers' hearts are opened to the evangelistic message; the latter takes on the marks of liberal and liberationist strains of mission. Social service is promoted as the way to go because it *works*. Churches engaged in social service vis-à-vis social action *grow* more.

charts and graphs and formulas. It seemed simple enough: make disciples of all people. There was, of course, the accommodationistic social gospel of time warps past, which advocated a mere presence with the people and belittled historic evangelism;[32] yet this was blatant heresy in the minds of most evangelical Christians and dismissed as such.

But when the movement came along, one of its initial actions was to deal with the question of what constitutes a disciple. And it did so in the only way it knew how—by measurement. How can we quantify discipleship? they asked. And the answer was, by linking it with the fruits of the faith, most notably responsible church membership. To believe or not to believe is not the question. It's too slippery. Too elusive. Too, in short, unquantifiable. But responsible church membership, the Growthmen sighed, *that* we can measure. So, various quantifiable behaviors were concocted to define this faith: regularity of church and cell-group attendance, percentage of giving, use of spiritual gifts, etc.[33]

Not surprisingly, this emphasis has given rise to much criticism, the most strident being the claim that to attempt to measure faith by such outward, behavioral criteria is not wholly dissimilar to the mind-set of the Pharisees of Bible times.[34] The mission of the

---

32. Originally, church growth's evangelistic mandate was fashioned as a counterinfluence to this accommodationistic social gospel—the "cup of water in the name of Jesus" school of mission so decried by McGavran and the others early on. Ironically, however, church growth has become largely accommodationistic, both in foreign fields and here at home. The HUP, as it plays out in the Third World, endorses alignment with the culture, not separation from it. And in America, consider the businesslike emphasis on the bottom line; the marketing paradigm (retailing religion); the obsessive interest in action, not theory, in results, not doctrine; the "find a need and meet it" credo that anchors the church growth mantra. The quintessence: what the people want is what the church should give them. Indeed, if it's anything, American church growth is Madison Avenue at prayer.

33. A classic text on measuring faith, penned by Arn the Elder and Arn the Younger, is *The Master's Plan for Making Disciples*.

34. See T. Raabe, "Quantifying the Unquantifiable." (Real scholars footnote themselves whenever possible, too.)

---

church, these critics say, is thus reduced to sociologically defined and measurable good works, not the conversion of sinners from unbelief to faith.

Also emerging almost from the get-go has been the *Bellum Grammaticae* (The War of Grammar) over how the Great Commission should be parsed. The main verb is to "make disciples." This is done, all agree, by "going," "baptizing,"[35] and "teaching them to observe all things I have commanded you." The Growthmen apply a law-oriented coloration to the last participle, i.e., that disciples are to be taught gradually how to live good Christian lives. Critics interpret the phrase to mean that disciples will confess and believe "all things."

The Homogeneous Unit Principle and the "Rabies Radicalorum"

Perhaps no issue in the theology of church growth sends up the red flags as readily as the homogeneous unit principle does.[36] McGavran, speaking *ex sociologica*, set down the kernel of the doctrine: "Men like to become Christians without crossing racial, linguistic, or class barriers."[37] Blacks evangelizing blacks; whites, whites; Orientals, Orientals; Hungabunga tribesmen, Hungabunga tribesmen; Yuppies, Yuppies; and so forth. People like joining churches where the members look, act, and talk the way *they* do.[38] This is quintes-

---

35. Search as one may, one will not find reference in church growth material to the sacrament of baptism as a viable way to make disciples. Baptism, after all, is (1) a Negotiable, and (2) a theologically limiting doctrine, especially when taken in concert with the object of the Great Commission, "all nations," which would include infants. Rather than take a stand that might tick off some Lutherans, Episcopalians, and Catholics, thus jeopardizing its atheological basis, church growth ignores it completely.

36. The name is widely attributed to McGavran, but in reality is named in honor of its discoverer, Indian mystic Homer "the Genius" U. Nitt. Nitt, upon learning that his name was to be so enshrined, reacted with passion, refusing to grant McGavran the necessary permission. However, when McGavran unveiled his alternative—"similitudinously defined contextualized evangelistic constituency"—the sage reluctantly relented.

37. Donald A. McGavran, *Understanding Church Growth*, rev. ed. (Grand Rapids: Eerdmans, 1980), 223.

38. As television commentator John McLaughlin is wont to say, this is "a key grasp of the obvious."

---

sential *solus practicus.*

Homogenists, as the principle's adherents came to be known, rallied behind McGavran's "mosaic" pronouncement[39]—"Since men like to become Christians without crossing barriers, the first task among the two billion [yet to be evangelized] is an evangelism designed to multiply churches in each new piece of the magnificent mosaic"[40]—and gave the principle wings. The attendant doctrines were systematized;[41] a biblical justification was constructed;[42] and the doctrine was trotted out for feedback from the field.

What trotted back was outrage. Critics, who formed a loose association called the Heterogenists, let loose a torrent of inflammatory epithets; the Homogenists were called racists,[43] narrow-minded exclusivists, and psychological manipulators, to name three. One critic, Gibson Winter, wailed that homogeneous churches are an "unholy alliance[44] of religious and racial segregation, an alliance whose real purpose is to preserve insulated residential communities."[45]

The bases of the Heterogenists' complaint were several: the belief that the church, more than any other entity in the world, must demonstrate the internal reconciliation of like and unlike people; the belief that the gospel must include a cultural imperative to break down racist and classist barriers; and the contention that the homo-

---

39. Not to be confused with the pronouncements of Moses.

40. Quoted in C. Peter Wagner, *Our Kind of People: The Ethical Dimensions of Church Growth in America* (Atlanta: John Knox, 1979), 20–21.

41. The doctrines of "peoples movements," "evangelizing the masses, not the classes," and "redemption and lift" are all closely associated with the homogeneous unit principle.

42. The Holy Bible, passim.

43. This was back when the term meant something.

44. To be distinguished from the Wheaton-Dallas-Pasadena Holy Alliance and the New York-Washington-Scottdale Holy Alliance, both of which were referred to later in the conflict as "*un*holy alliances" by the respective opposing sides.

45. Quoted in Wagner, *Our Kind of People,* 26.

The Ultimate Church

geneous principle implicitly endorses segregation, discrimination, and apartheid.

When these Heterogenists joined ranks with the "New *Kulturkampfers*,"[46] the age of the "rabies radicalorum"[47] was ushered in. The New *Kulturkampfers* argued that omitting the ethical dimensions of the Christian life—living in peace and harmony with others—from the initial message is, in effect, cheating the new convert. That person becomes a Christian and then all of a sudden there is this missionary in his face telling him he can't be a racist or a classist anymore.[48] They called it "cheap grace."

The polemic was elevated, and war broke out.[49] Magazine pages seethed with excoriating invective; protest songs were written; marches were organized.[50] The pilpul was palpable. One singular aspect of the altercation lay in the curious coincidence that both sides employed the same battle cry to fire up their troops—Liston Pope's famed observation: "Eleven o'clock on Sunday morning is the most

---

46. Many of whom occupied office space in *Sojourners* and *The Other Side* editorial rooms, as well as at Mennonite headquarters.

47. "Rage of the radicals."

48. This concept is used in modified form as a carrot to draw unbelievers to worship in some churches, most notably Schuller's Crystal Cathedral. Visitors sit in the opulent sanctuary, rhapsodize over the mid-nave fountains, listen to the celebrity testimonial, hear the be-all-that-you-can-be homily, and decide that Christianity must be pretty good stuff, so they enroll in the pastor's class. Only then do they learn that there are these things called sin and repentance involved in it all.

49. Called "The Logomachy" and "The War of the Words," this conflict remained largely verbal, aside from one unseemly incident at a Society of Biblical Literature conference at which some radicals, taking the "rabies radicalorum" literally, bit the legs of some Fuller profs.

50. The most dramatic of which occurred when Homogenists staged a coordinated march on mainline and radical headquarters around the nation, chanting slogans and waving their fists. The most popular slogan: "HUP, two, three, four; heterogeneity makes us sore." The unintentional result at at least one mainline center—United Methodist headquarters in Nashville—was that officials viewed with horror this militaristic metaphor and tried to remove "Onward, Christian Soldiers" from their hymnal.

---

segregated hour in the week."[51] But each used it to different effect. To the Heterogenists it was a gushing of vituperation, while the Homogenists pumped their fists into the air and cried, "Right on!"

From the ferocity of such conflict, however, has come the window for rapprochement. Both the Homogenists and Heterogenists have sought common ground and are on the brink of effecting the Third Great Amelioration.[52] Leading Homogenist spokesman C. Peter Wagner has called homogeneity "descriptive not normative . . . phenomonological, not theological,"[53] and has exhibited a conspicuous reluctance to flaunt the buzzwords in recent writings. On the Heterogenist side, René Padilla, an outspoken critic of the principle, has written that it "may have to be accepted as a necessary, but provisional, measure for the sake of the fulfillment of Christ's mission."[54]

Recent Trends

Research, of course, is an ever-growing stream. More facts are gathered, more principles deduced, more church growth seminars conducted.[55] And as Growthmen analyze the evidence, they will ascertain more areas where growth can be effected. One such area may be the charismatic movement. At least one leading Growthman,[56] having denounced it previously, has turned volte-face to endorse it. The reason? Signs and wonders work. Not so much in a charismatic way, though he believes they do there, too, but in a util-

---

51. Quoted in Wagner, *Our Kind of People*, 25.
52. Too many more of these "great ameliorations" and church growth will be indistinguishable from generic evangelicalism. And then where would we be—me, especially?
53. Wagner, *Church Growth and the Whole Gospel*, 167.
54. René Padilla, "The Unity of the Church and the Homogeneous Principle," in Wilbert R. Shenk, ed., *Exploring Church Growth* (Grand Rapids: Eerdmans, 1983), 301.
55. The cry "Next year in Pasadena" resonates through the halls of many growing churches.
56. C. Peter Wagner.

itarian way. They grow churches and therefore should be used.[57]

Also, a consolidation of growth forces seems to loom on the horizon. The complaint has come down from the Holy City[58] that pastors across the country are claiming status as Growthmen, whereas in reality all they are really doing is sending out a greeter team or mowing their church lawns regularly.[59] Thus the very definition of church growth has been fuzzified. The Growthmen, for their part, insist that the movement is defined by subscription to the principles emanating from the Pasadena curia alone, and all posturing to the contrary is counterfeit. Look for a *quatenus* [60] subscription versus *quia*[61] subscription debate in years ahead as church growth pulls in the reins.

As for what else the future holds, who knows? New chapters in the church growth story are being written daily.[62] We can only wait and see and hope other historians will view the events with the perspicacity and objectivity displayed in this rendering.

---

57. Lucky for new converts, the "Stylite" sect has not seen rapid growth. They'd be sitting on flagpoles for the rest of their lives.

58. You know where.

59. You don't have to enroll at Fuller to learn that.

60. "Insofar as" (i.e., one eclectically chooses the doctrines one wishes to employ).

61. "Because" (i.e., one subscribes to all of it because it is true).

62. Or at least books are. The number of volumes rolling off church growth presses is mind-boggling.

63. Dave Barry, passim.

Soil Testing on the Sand

It used to be you just piled the youth group onto a bus, trucked them down to the beach, and told them to "share Christ." Divide and conquer. Read the booklet to people. Pray. And everything would turn out all right. Leave the results to God and all that.

But that was in the ancient days of unenlightened methodology. Now, of course, it's all passé. Rendered scientifically invalid because of poor results. In short, the numbers just aren't there.

But let's be whimsical, if we may, for a few moments and imagine the beach evangelism outreach effort as it would unfold under the new criteria, taking into account the receptivity-resistance factor and its attendant rubric, soil testing.

It is Saturday. Sunny. Eight-foot swells from the southwest. And the throngs of sunworshipers are joined by five packed school buses that have pulled into the parking lot of a popular beach and disgorged 250 excited young people, hyped into an enthusiastic spirit to evangelize and led by the doughty presence of one Commander Beachhead. As the troops descend onto the sand, Beachhead repairs to base command (a specially equipped Winnebago in the parking lot), where he stands with his able adjutant, Sam Simpson, before a bank of television monitors—closed-circuit cameras have been mounted on each lifeguard tower—to take in the action. But things are not right. The monitors are unkind, and Beachhead, professionally trained in the evangelistic sciences, becomes more distraught with every passing moment. Finally he can hold it in no longer. We pick up the action:

—I question the efficacy of that, Simpson.

—What, sir?

—Why do we have a discipling unit at the jetty?

—Video on Tower 16, Randy. . . . Ah yes, I see. DU-14F.

—Right. Why are they there?

—Well, I suppose it's because I told them to work the jetty, sir. You see, I took the number of towers and divided it into the number of discipling units and assigned them to the various areas. That way we get an equal distribution of evangelistic force. We saturate the beach.

—That's great, Simpson. Just great. I go over the mountains for a two-week seminar and the whole ministry goes to pot. Haven't you learned *anything* since you've come on board, man?

—Well . . . uh . . .

—Putting a unit at the jetty is an obviously sinful allocation of evangelistic energy. I thought you said you tested this soil. Look at those waves, Simpson. Eight-foot peaks. Left-hand curl. Tube city. Now look at those surfers. Wha'd'ya see?

—Uh . . . surfers, sir.

— *Happy* surfers, Simpson. And happy surfers are unreceptive surfers. We could bring all 125 units down on them and still only get three, maybe four, conversions. Let's move DU-14F to a receptive field.

—Uh, where exactly, commander?

—Well, let's take a look. . . . We've got action at Tower 4, Simpson.

—Zoom on Tower 4, Randy.

—Now *that's* a receptive field.

—It looks as if somebody's in trouble, sir. See, they're dragging that guy out of the surf, they're laying him on the beach, they're administering . . .

—Anybody can see that, Simpson. But what do you see when you look at it through "church growth eyes"?

—Uh . . . I don't know, sir.

—You don't know. Sad. Very sad. Simpson, some of the most elementary research in the science shows that people are most receptive to the gospel immediately after a transitional period in their lives. "Narrowly escaping death by drowning," while not addressed per se on the Holmes-Rahe Stress Test, would have to come in at a pretty healthy 50 or so out of 100. We should have a unit standing by to evangelize that guy when he comes to. Winning the winnable while they're winnable, Simpson. Read my lips. Win-ning the win-na . . .

—He's coming to, sir.

—And our guys are standing around like a bunch of doofuses. Get a unit on the scene, Simpson.

—Right, sir. . . . Base to DU-4G. Base to DU-4G. Come in, DU-4G.

—And, for heaven's sake, get a unit—no, make that two—on the family. They're standing there, ripe as can be, and our guys are nowhere to be found. "Change in family member's health" is a 44. Not as good as if the guy had bit the big one—that's a 63—but we've got to take our opportunities. . . . What in blazes is going on at Tower 8, Simpson? Simpson!

—Uh . . .

—Tower 8, Simpson. Who is *that* guy?

—Oh, that's Fernstal Babington III, sir. DU-9E.

—What's he doing in a three-piece suit? This is the beach!

—He usually handles our courtroom ministry, commander.

—That's got to be an E-1-C cultural jump, using Hunter's Sevenfold Typology. I consider this to be a direct affront to doctrine, Simpson.

—Doctrine, sir? What does doctrine have to do with evangelism? I instruct our discipling units to stay as far away from doctrine as possible, commander. Social relationships bring people to Christ, not doctrine. That is basic, elementary, primary church growth teach—

—Not that kind of doctrine, Simpson. I'm talking about the homogeneous unit principle.

—Oh, violation of the HUP? That *is* serious. What should I do?

—Get him to the acculturation trailer for a native customs makeover and "heart language" indoctrination.

—Right, sir. Base to DU-9E. Base to DU-9E. . . . Wait, sir! I'm getting emergency clearance from Nicole of DU-10B. Seems she's got a near-decision at Tower 9, sir. She's got the target individual at minus-3 on the Engel Scale—"personal problem recognition"—but can't get him over the hump.

—Tower 9, eh? Let me check it out. Ah yes, that Tom Cruise look-alike must be the target individual. Question her on methodology.

—She indicates she asked him to dinner and he told her to scram.

—What? No, no. Evangelistic method, Simpson. Evangelistic method. Give me that mike. . . . Base to DU-10B. Come in, DU-10B. What is going on here, Simpson? Do you read, DU-10B? Why doesn't she answer?

—She's begun hugging him, sir.

—Hugging him! . . . Nicole, you pick up that walkie-talkie right this minute!

—Holding the resistance lightly, eh, commander?

—This is no time for jokes, Simpson. Call in a perfecting unit.

—But the target individual hasn't even made a decision yet, sir.

—Not for the target individual, Simpson! For Nicole!

—Base to PU-32. Immediate perfecting duty required at Tower 9. Base to . . . I've got an emergency call from the acculturation trailer, sir.

—What is it?

—It's Fernstal Babington III, sir. He has rejected the "heart language" indoctrination. He refuses to use the word *stoked* in every other sentence.

—Sheesh. . . . This is just great, Simpson. Just great. We'll be lucky if we get any numbers today.

—Oh, we've already got five 2-P conversions and twenty-one near-decisions, according to preliminary tallies, sir.

—And rejections. How many of those?
—Six hundred thirty, sir.
—Poor souls. We'll have to leave those to God.

Quantifying the Unquantifiable

Wouldn't you know it? Just when somebody comes up with a crackerjack program that really works, it never fails that somebody somewhere is going to take a shot at it.

Take the church growth movement, for example. Here a group of conscientious people come up with some great ideas for growing churches and fulfilling the Great Commission. They set it down on charts and graphs and can't-miss universal principles, and then they sell it to a number-hungry and member-starved clergy who gobble it up and put it into practice, and—eureka!—what happens but those number-hungry and member-starved preachers' churches begin to grow like gangbusters.

They explode! Their growth rates climb off the charts. Hundreds and even thousands of people flock through their doors, and their ministries become throbbing dynamos of ecclesiastical health.

But then, wouldn't you know it, along come some *liberals* who find some itty-bitty, picayune thing they don't like about this robust and vibrant church health, and they accuse the church growth people of being in it just for the numbers. "You're playing the numbers game," they say. "All you want to do is hit the people with a quick shot of Jesus and then sign them up on your roles. You're into quantity, not quality."

So, back in their faces come the church growth people saying that no, indeed, they are not in the numbers game. They care about quality, too. And to prove it, they decide to put some punch into their numbers.

Now, you have to understand something about church growth people. They're really sociologists dressed up to look like theologians, and the thing that really makes them tick is when they can measure people's behaviors. They are heavily into quantification. They have ratios and formulae and charts and graphs for *everything*. They like making up ten-step programs to make such-and-such happen or eighteen-reason lists why this or that occurs or forty-four surefire ways to make people do one thing or another. They're how-to types who want to make sure they can measure how it went.

So when they decide to put some quality into their quantity, it is only consistent with their calling that they will want to quantify that quality, and that is, unfortunately, tough to do in this case because the quality they are concerned with is unquantifiable.

It is faith. Faith is the object of the Great Commission. Faith is the thing they are trying to put into people's hearts, and unfortunately you can't see faith. Observe, chart, plot, graph, analyze, scrutinize, and count all you want, you cannot get a statistical handle on the thing.

However, every instance of faith does have as a requisite by-product the fruits of that faith. And fruits, anyhow, you can see. So the church growth people decided: We'll beat this no-quality rap. We'll show those liberals. We'll quantify the fruits.

And because the Great Commission is all about "making disciples"—and not just about getting people to tramp to the front of the tent—they said, we'll get it down in good, solid, observable terms what that sought–after discipleship entails, and we'll measure that.

So they decided that a disciple was in reality a "responsible church member," one who is incorporated into the institutional church and displays the fruits of the faith through various observable behaviors, including, among other things, feeling a sense of spiritual growth and progress, utilizing one's spiritual gift in some way, being involved in a cell group, making x number of new friends every year, and tithing. One who stacks up favorably in these areas is a responsible church member, exhibiting the fruits of the faith in sufficient quantity—ergo, a disciple.

While this has shut the mouths of some critics, wouldn't you know it, along comes another disgruntled old grouch—me—who isn't even satisfied with this. My quibble is with the criteria: Are they thorough enough? Are they an accurate and reliable measurement of the faith they purportedly serve as fruits of? In short, is it possible to beat the system?

Let's examine tithing, for example, one of the behaviors. Measuring giving only measures giving. It tells us that the giver gives. But does it measure what it purports to measure, i.e., faith? Why does the tither tithe? Does he expect material reward? Is he really a health-and-wealther disguised in a cheap suit?

You see the problem, of course. The criteria are soft, quality-wise. They leave us stranded in sociological limbo. We don't really know if the guy's a disciple or not.

If we are going to pull the Great Commission out of the believer's heart and put it into his actions, and if the focus is to be the building of the Institutional Church rather than the *Una Sancta,* then we can ill afford nebulous and ambiguous measurement criteria as our gauge.

We need some tougher rules!

But what? Let's look at the criterion of feeling a sense of spiritual growth and progress. This criterion deals with Christian education. That's how one grows and progresses spiritually. But the most irresponsible member in the church can put on a responsible pose. He can sit politely in the back of Bible class noshing on fellowship-hour donuts and slurping coffee when he should be jotting notes in his Bible. And who knows how many days at a time he sleeps right through his morning quiet time? The criterion is eminently beatable.

It needs teeth. What about the Bible he totes to church? Is it a zippered, monogrammed, extensively magic-markered deluxe edition without a thumb index? In short, is it the Bible of a responsible church member? And when a passage is cited, is he on it in a flash—even if it is in the Minor Prophets? Or is he flipping through the table of contents to find Matthew? Obviously, the existent guidelines for this criterion are far too vague.

Or, let's look at making new friends in the church. The idea is that a person who makes new friends is in the church to stay, not a flash-in-the-pan sort who whips up a testimonial, gets his name on the roll, and then spends his Sunday mornings tossing back brewskis and watching the early game of the NFL doubleheader. No, he's got new friends who will make sure he's there listening to the sermon, who will get him on various committees, see to it that he uses his spiritual gift(s), etc. In short, he will be *responsible*.

That's the theory. But there are mitigating factors. What really constitutes a friend? How does the disciple know that the guy schmoozing with him in the coffee line is really a friend? Will he lend him money without interest? Will he *give* him money? Will he give him a job? Will he cover for him the next time he ditches meeting night?

And this doesn't even take into consideration the alleged disciple. Because, let's face it, some people don't really have a gift for making friends. There are personal issues to think of, like a belligerent personality, terminal halitosis, or severe body odor. Maybe he thinks he's got the spiritual gift of prophecy and stalks the narthex in some old pauper's rags, saying, "Thus saith the Lord," to everybody he meets. He may be as responsible as a deacon taking his daughter and her date to a drive-in, but he isn't going to make many new friends.

Get the idea? Or, take another of the responsibleness criteria, that of having a task or role in the church appropriate to one's spiritual gift. What this really means is: Does the person attend meetings? Not a very definitive measurement, that. What we should ask is, *How many* meetings does the person attend? Not only that, but what sort of attitude does the person exhibit when he is there? Is the person a picture of saintly enthusiasm, contributing to the proceedings with bright, uplifting comments, or is he using the time to clandestinely compute his fantasy football league stats?

Obviously, a lot more thinking must go into this before a code of foolproof criteria can be arrived at.

But if we truly want to get serious about measuring responsible church membership, we could start by going for guidance to the experts in the field, the people who exuded the quintessence of responsibleness, responsible church members par excellence. The best. The most conscientious of them all.

The Pharisees.

But then, wouldn't you know it, somebody would probably get bent out of shape over that, too.

Holding the Resistance Lightly

"And now, we come to our last few items, candidates. I appreciate your patience, as this session has dragged on for upwards of an hour. And I trust the Holy Spirit will work in your hearts as you consider the many exciting ministry possibilities open to you. In addition to the twenty-two suburban megachurch opportunities you have just seen, there are three other positions—I would term them rare and rewarding challenges for the fresh-from-seminary candidate—that I would like to show you now. Slide, please, Burt.

"This is opportunity number twenty-three, candidates. Actually, this is the 'before' shot of the sanctuary. Note the majestic spires, the sandstone exterior. Next slide. . . . This is the interior. Ornate stained-glass windows. Raised pulpit with canopy. Clerestory windows. Altar and reredos of unmatched and meticulous workmanship. The church dates back to 1867. Oldest church in the city. Slide, please, Burt. . . . This is the 'after' shot. The 'Victory Bar and Grill' sign has, of course, since been replaced with 'New Hope Community Church.' Actually, this is the after 'after' shot. Slide, please. . . . *This* is the 'after' shot. . . . What's that, Ken? . . . Yes, it is nothing but a vacant lot. Arson. Burned to the ground last year. No one was apprehended, although the youth group, which has ties to the local Crips gang, is largely suspected. Next, Burt. . . . This is a picture of the congregation. . . . Yes, you're correct, Jason. A wide-angle lens was *not* necessary to fit them all in. New Hope Commu-

nity has only forty-five members, and . . . what's that, Martha? . . .
Yes, the challenges for homogeneous groupings are significant.
Blacks, Hispanics, Italians, Poles, Germans, Irish, poor whites.
Social tensions run high in the area. But on the bright side, there are,
at last count, thirty-two homogeneous extension ministries possible.
(*Laughs*) Naturally, as in most changing neighborhoods, the original
membership has long since fled to the suburbs. . . . Other challenges,
Jason? . . . Well, yes, there are many. Unemployment is high. Hous-
ing inadequate. Recreational facilities are nonexistent. Marital insta-
bility rears its ugly head in a plethora of single-parent families. Many
juveniles are in trouble with the law by age thirteen. And the area is
riddled with crime—the elderly are afraid to leave their high-rises
after 5:00 P.M.—4:00 P.M. in the winter. Clearly, New Hope Community calls for a candidate with a heart of love and service, one who is
willing to accept the realities of urban decay and is challenged to
minister to hurting people. . . . Pay? . . . Good question, Mark. At
last count, New Hope Community had a grand total of two tithers.
Its existence is solely due to subsidy from denominational headquarters. The ministerial salary reflects this economic reality—$14,000
per annum. But don't let that sway you. Service under the Cross is a
rewarding service, people. You can grow immeasurably in faith and
love. Okay, Burt, next. . . .

"And here, candidates, we have opportunity number twenty-
four. Notice the simple clapboard exterior, the spare little bell tower.
It's very beautiful in a rural sort of way. Slide, Burt. . . . And this is
the interior, equally spare. Hymn boards. Unpadded pews. An electronic organ with a tremolo stop that can shake the windows. Worship here is intense, candidates, albeit somewhat lacking on the quality index. Every hymn sounds as if it's being sung by seventy-five
Roseanne Barrs. (*Laughs*) Next, Burt. . . . And this is the congregational group shot. . . . No, Clara, the name of the church is not Meth-
uselah Dutch Reformed Church. (*Laughs*) It's Faith, set in quintessential rural America, replete with all the problems thereof. A very
static community. Nobody moving in; everybody under thirty, and
small farmers who have gone bust, moving out. . . . Yes, Joshua, life
is pretty settled for these folks. And as for excitement, the most

thrilling thing that happened last year was when Marna Devries dropped two stitches in one day at the Phoebe Quilting Circle. (*Laughs*) . . . Church growth potential? Good point, Sarah. There is absolutely none here. Biological growth potential—nil; transfer growth potential—nil; conversion growth potential—nil, although there *are* three town atheists living together above the feed co-op. . . . Yes, Martin, I'd agree. The church pathology is old-age; Faith Dutch Reformed is on life-support, and a flatline is inevitable. And with their set ways comes an exclusivity that will require the pastor's particular attention. Faith has only three surnames on the entire church roster—Van Dyke, Vander Linden, and Vanderhoof. . . . No, Jason, all the Vanderhorsts attend another little country church seven miles to the west. . . . But there are some pluses. Burt, please. . . . The adjacent cemetery has plenty of room for expansion. (*Laughs*) . . . Yes, Sam, it is ironic that the back door opens directly onto the first row of gravestones. Gives new meaning to the term 'backdoor loss.' . . .

"But, lest we get too sportive here, people, bear in mind that the members of Faith need pastoral support just as much as do the members of your generic megachurch. These people hurt, too, folks. Many are elderly; some are bed-ridden. They expect regular visits; they want traditional pastoral care; they need encouragement, absolution, prayer, counseling, handholding, etc. They want a *Seelsorger,* a curer of souls. But don't worry about it. There'll be plenty of time for it. After all, you won't have anything else to do. And as for pay, . . . I'm surprised there are no questions about salary. . . . Anybody? . . . Well, three years ago they went off a monetary scale. The pastoral salary now stands at a side of beef per year and all the vegetables and dairy products you can eat. Ha, ha! . . . Now, any other questions about Faith Dutch Reformed?

"Okay, then we move on to our last ministry opportunity. Burt? . . . This field is burgeoning with challenge, candidates. As you can see, there is no actual church building in our first slide. Can anybody tell me where this photo was taken? Come on, students, give it a shot. No takers? Well, this is the wilds of the upper Amazon basin. Slide Burt. . . . And these are the people of this mission field. The Zambahooey tribe. Can anybody identify the items in each of these braves' right hands? . . . What's the problem, people? Cat got your tongue? . . . They're spears! And in their left hands are shields. And on their faces is war paint. You no doubt have heard of the two missionaries who were martyred here last year. Well, amidst all the publicity, there is one item that has been routinely overlooked. Who can tell me what that is? . . . Why am I getting no response, folks? Tell you what, if you answer the question, I'll swing a two-year internship at Hollywood Presbyterian, ha, ha! . . . Anyone? . . . Well, what's been lost is the fact that those two missionaries converted a core group of a dozen tribesmen before giving their lives for Christ. We need a replacement, one courageous soul who will walk intrepidly among the heathen and build the church in the Amazon basin. The homogeneous factor is sky-high, although there are grave doubts about receptivity—the Zambahooey come in at a minus-five on the McGavran Resistance-Receptivity Scale. But nowhere are the challenges for ministry greater. . . .

"Now, any questions on the Amazon mission? None? Well, any questions in general on any of the twenty-five opportunities? Well, for a group that was initially so inquisitive, you've suddenly gone remarkably silent. At any rate, let me conclude by encouraging all of you to think and pray about these mission possibilities. Ask the Spirit's guidance as you consider where your aptitudes and abilities can best be used; where the Lord's kingdom can best be served with your talents. . . . And if there are no further questions, I'll ask Burt to hit the lights. Burt?"

Burt hit the lights. All of the candidates had long since left the room.

Church Growth in
Historical Perspective

Moses and the
Spiritual Gifts Inventory

(Scene: *A tent in the land of Midian. Moses, a Hebrew in self-imposed exile, has just returned from Mount Horeb troubled and exhausted. There was a burning bush. There was a high-powered conversation with the Lord. And although he was initially reluctant to accept it, there was the mind-boggling charge to lead his people out of bondage in Egypt. Now it is bugging him something fierce. After all, this didn't jibe at all with the results of a Spiritual Gifts Inventory his wife, Zipporah, had administered before he took his sheep out a few days earlier. They had been intent on discovering his gifts and finding him a place in God's plan. He scored high in helps and administration. And now this. It is devastating. After some shilly-shallying around, he drops this bomb on his wife.*)[1]

—You're supposed to do what?!
—Um, lead the children of Israel out of Egypt, I guess.
—You have *got* to be kidding, Moses. You?
—That's what he said. From a burning bush. "I will send you to Pharaoh that you may bring forth my people, the sons of Israel, out of Egypt." Those were his exact words.

---

1. This conversation occurred between verses 19 and 20 of Exodus 4.

—That's rich, Moses. You? A leader? A prophet? You don't have any of the right spiritual qualities. Zilch. You came in at a three on the leadership section of your spiritual gifts inventory. You have the gifts of helps and administration. You'd be perfect in some bureaucratic post. But leadership? No way!

—Well, to be fair, I haven't really experimented with that gift, Zip. I've really never tried leading a couple million people out of bondage before.

—You can't even lead sheep. What were you doing way over by Mount Horeb in the first place? Grass around here not good enough for you?

—Yeah, well . . . mfgrbphcrrmph.

—You're mumbling again, Moses. Leaders are vibrant, motivational speakers. And you? You don't exactly have the gift of gab—spiritual or otherwise. You scored in negative numbers on "exhortation," and you checked "completely disagree" on statements like "It seems people generally follow my advice." And what about your temper? You wouldn't be out here in this no-man's land if you hadn't upped and offed that Egyptian taskmaster. Leaders have a little more control than that, Moses. Besides, those guys in Pharaoh's court hate your guts. You try to lead the Hebrews out of Egypt and they're liable to off *you*, not to mention what they'll do to your people.

—I've tried to get out of it, Zip. I've examined my feelings on this thing.

—Well, at least you did that right. That's crucial to gift discovery.

—I would absolutely *hate* leading those people.

—Well, did you tell him that?

—Sure I did. I trotted out every excuse I could think of. "Who am I," I said, "that I should go to Pharaoh and bring the sons of Israel out of Egypt?"

—Imagine, a guy with your low self-esteem leading that big bunch of crybabies out of Egypt. You come whimpering up to those Hebrews, they won't believe a word you say.

—I told him that, too.

—And?

—He showed me how to do some miracles that would convince them. Staffs turning into snakes, hands going leprous, stuff like that.

—Those Egyptians are no slouches when it comes to miracles, either, Moses. They'd score off the board if we gave them the SGI. What else? Did you tell him you can't talk worth beans?

—Absolutely! I said I was heavy of speech and of tongue. My exact words. Finally I laid it all on the line. I pleaded. I begged. "Send some other person," I said. Zip, this is bugging the daylights out of me.

—And what'd he say?

—He said he'd send Aaron with me.

—Aaron! Now there's a guy who can talk. He was way up there in the speaking gifts.

—I don't know, Zip. This is bad. Real bad!

—You're telling me.

—Maybe I should take the test again.

—What would that prove?

—A lot of people get totally different scores every time they take it. I was kind of bummed that first time. With that Egyptian thing hanging over my head and a couple of weeks wandering in the desert and everything.

—Oh, Moses, this is embarrassing. What are you going to do?

—I guess I'll do it. What choice do I have?

—I've got it, Moses. Ask for another meeting. Go up to Mount Horeb again. Show him your SGI.

—No, I don't think he'd go for that. He was pretty definite about the whole thing.

—But why? You don't have any of the necessary spiritual gifts. You don't feel good about it. You probably won't get any sort of confirmation from that bunch of whiners in Goshen. Why, Moses?

—The only thing I can figure is that God chooses "what is foolish in the world to shame the wise, . . . what is weak in the world to shame the strong, . . . what is low and despised in the world, even things that are not, to bring to nothing things that are, so that no human being might boast in the presence of God."

—Oh, come on, Moses. That's not how it works.

—No, *you* come on, Zip. Let's go back to Egypt. . . . Say, by the way, could you circumcise Gershom for me?

—Why?

—I didn't score too well on the spiritual gift of knife-handling.

Zeke Sonabuzi and the Church Growth Consultant

(Scene: *Babylon, sixth century* B.C., *among the exiles. A man, clad in the purest silk finery, stalks impatiently in front of the window of his penthouse suite of the Tel Abib Hilton and peers out over the river Chebar awaiting his first appointment of the morning. He is Hananiah Jackson, church growth consultant, Children of Israel, dispatched from denominational headquarters to this remote outpost of the faith, and he is teed-off. First, the red-eye camel train from Jerusalem didn't get in until 2 A.M. Second, there was this crazy man with hair all over his body and a crown on his head crawling on all fours and barking his head off below his window all night. And now this backwoods preacher, wouldn't you know it, is late. There is a knock at the door. Hananiah moves to open it. A bedraggled, filthy man, wretched and malodorous, tramps through the door to one of the two chairs situated near the window, where he stands. Hananiah follows. Once there, cheeks are kissed and pleasantries are exchanged, albeit with some reluctance on Hananiah's part. Both men sit, and the interview begins.*)

—Now, then, let's get started, shall we? Name?

—I am Ezekiel, son of Buzi.

—Let me get that down. . . . Son-a-buz-i. Zeke Sonabuzi. You a Levite, Zeke?

—I am a priest and the son of a priest.

—Okay . . . good. Now, turning to your church growth profile, I see you began your ministry here in 593 B.C., right?

—That is correct.

—And you immediately experienced heavy transfer growth. Is that right, Zeke?

—Yes. All who were exiled in 597 with Jehoiachin. Princes, mighty men of valor, captives, craftsmen, and smiths.

—Good, good. That kind of transfer growth is not unusual in satellite situations. . . . But I also see that since then, your growth has been confined to mere biological growth. Annual growth rate, 0.1 percent; decadal growth rate, 2 percent; very little bridging growth; E-0 evangelism type only; possible fellowship inflammation—all the trademark signs of koinonitis, fella. Have you analyzed this lack of growth, Zeke? Dissipated the fog, as it were?

—Well . . . uh . . . no, I guess not.

—I can tell you one problem I see right off the bat here.

—What's that?

—It's called hygiene. When's the last time you took a shower, friend? You reek!

—I was digging through the wall of my house last night as a symbolic gesture foretelling the ignominious escape attempt of Zedekiah and the children of Israel from a besieged Jerusalem.

—Digging through walls in the dead of night, eh? Is that typical of your ministry here?

—Earlier, for 390 consecutive days, I lay on my left side outside my house with my hands tied—a day for each year of Israel's sin.

—I see.

—After that, I lay forty straight days on my right side, a day for each year of Judah's sin.

—Uh-huh. I think I'm beginning to see why your church is not growing, Zeke. I'm curious, what is your philosophy of ministry?

—I am a watchman sent to warn the people that destruction is the inevitable consequence of their sins.

—Just as I thought. I bet your Spiritual Gifts Inventory comes in heavy on the prophecy side, eh?

—Thus says the Lord: "Doom has come upon you—you who dwell in the land. The time has come, the day is near; there is panic, not joy, upon the mountain."

—Uh . . . okay, Zeke. I get your drift.

—"I am about to pour out my wrath on you and spend my anger against you."

—Zeke, that's enough.

—"I will judge you according to your conduct and repay you for all your detestable practices."

—Zeke! Knock it off!

—Oh . . . uh . . . okay. Sorry.

—Zeke, you have got to chill out, man.

—But I'm a prophet! This is what I'm *supposed* to say.

—Sure, sure. You prophetic types are all the same. Amos and Hosea up north 150 years ago. Isaiah, Micah, Obadiah. But I'll tell you something, there was no church growth in those ministries. Doom and gloom do not put people in the pews. Preaching famine and death does not send them away happy.

—But I speak truth.

—Don't tell me. The old quality-versus-quantity argument, right? Calling the people back to faithfulness and all that. I've heard all the nongrowth excuses, Zeke, and they're cop-outs. They don't grow churches.

—But Israel must repent of its sins.

—We have a guy back in Jerusalem who's the same way, hitting the people with very outlandish stuff, fire and brimstone like you would not believe. And how does the city respond to his message? Do they break down the temple doors to get in to hear him? No way! They try to kill the guy. They throw him in prison.

—Must be Jeremiah.

—Depressed, gloomy, morose, negative, moody, low self-esteem, overly critical. A definite *im*possibility thinker.

—I know him.

—Why doesn't that surprise me? You two are poured from the same mold. When are you going to learn that that stuff just doesn't sell? We need positive preachers who will stimulate the positive emotions of the listeners, who will affirm and lift up the people and send them away feeling good. Get rid of this obsession for the prophetic stance and preach good news.

—But I don't preach *all* bad news.

—Oh, really?

—No. I tell the people some will be saved, some will be lifted out of destruction.

—I like that. That shows promise, Zeke.

—I have had inklings of a great vision, a vision of a great temple, perfectly symmetrical, where the Lord will be present in the midst of his people.

—All right!

—It will be five hundred cubits by five hundred cubits, with a hundred-cubit-long sanctuary and porticoes and vestibules and many side rooms and lots of steps and a big altar.

—Oh, this is inspiring! You're developing church growth eyes, Zeke. Don't forget surplus parking.

—I see magnificence and grandeur and majesty.

—Great! Terrific!

—And, above all, I see the Lord's restoration for his repentant people. I see salvation for those who repent of their sins and return to his ways.

—There you go again—sin, repentance, bad news. How many times do I have to tell you? Negatives do not work in church growth.

"The Silas and Paul
Praise Program"

(Scene: *A television studio somewhere in Rome, circa 61* A.D. *Two elevated curving ramps sprout from behind a picture of Jesus and wind toward center stage, where two long couches are set at a forty-five-degree angle, surrounded by lush ferns and local vegetation. At stage right huddles a group of squeaky-clean and immaculately coiffed young people clad in primary-color-coordinated attire, the females in chiffon dresses, the males in frilly tunics. Paired in couples, the singers, each holding a cordless microphone, take dry runs through the gestures they will execute during their numbers. At extreme right stage, behind the singers, their set lies in readiness—fake boulders set amid a fake stream that courses over a fake waterfall into a fake lake. Snippets of orchestral music burst over the sound system as technicians fine-tune the accompaniment track for the night's numbers. At stage left, the announcer runs over his notes. Behind him is a facade with large picture windows, through which appear artistic representations of the Forum, the Imperial Palaces, and the Circus Maximus.*

(*At extreme left stage three banks of tunic-clad scribes, all sitting behind desks, scribble furiously. Runners appear constantly, delivering epistles to the scribblers, carrying other rolled parchments away. Lackeys scurry about setting props, plumping pillows, dusting ferns. Suddenly, the studio is thrown into darkness. Numerous spotlights crisscross the studio audience and dance across the stage. A theme song blares from huge onstage speakers.)*

ANNOUNCER (*excitedly*): And now, live from Rome, it's time for S-A-P-P-P! "The Silas and Paul Praise Pro-o-ogram-m-m!" (*Spotlights come to rest in two foci at the top of each ramp.*) He-e-e-ere's Silas and Paul-l-l!

(Silas and Paul enter respective ramps at a gallop—Silas on left, Paul on right—their robes flowing, their faces bright with joy. They canter to center stage where, upon meeting, they shake hands, embrace, and then, turning to the audience, throw their arms up in triumph to acknowledge the thunderous applause.)

PAUL: Thank you, folks! Thank you, thank you! (*To Silas*) What a crowd, eh, Si?

SILAS (*shaking head in awe*): It's beautiful, Paul. Rome! The world's capital! Springtime! Abundant Christian living at its very best.

PAUL (*clapping hands and turning to audience*): And you, you wonderful, marvelous people of Rome, how are you this beautiful Roman evening? (*Tumultuous applause*) Ready to give the Devil a licking? (*Huge cheers*) Have we got a terrific show for you tonight, folks. James the Just is here from Jerusalem to share what is happening in his ministry. Timothy is dropping by a little later to fellowship on the great, *exciting* things that are going on in his life. Silas will be updating you on the upcoming World Tour IV, now less than a year away. We'll be reading letters from some of you wonderful viewers (*turns to banks of scribes with outstretched arm*)—our very own "Holy Scribblers" are standing by waiting to counsel the hurting with an epistle for successful living—and as always, the SAPPP Singers will be blessing us with song. (*Turns to waterfall tableaux.*) Isn't that right, Corny? (*Lead singer bows, smiles hugely.*) But first, a little business. Si?

SILAS (*standing stage left, beside a large drawing of a fund-raising thermometer*): Folks, we've been terrifically blessed on our journeys. Derbe, Lystra, Troas, Philippi, Athens, Corinth—we've been there; we've fellowshiped; we've preached and shared and spread the message; and your love gifts have sent us. (*Shouts of "All right!" "Right on!" etc., come from set.*) But we have a problem. (*Cut to extreme close-up of Silas.*) World Tour IV to Spain and the rest of the known world is in desperate financial difficulty. We need your help. (*Turns to thermometer.*) Right now we are thousands of denarii short of our goal. Please give prayer to becoming a partner with us on World Tour IV. Only a few denarii—a hundred or fifty or twenty-five or twenty or ten—anything you feel led to give. (*Cut to Paul seated on the couch.*)

PAUL: And with any love gift of a hundred denarii we would like you to have this colorful T-shirt. (*Holds T-shirt front to camera.*) It says, "Silas and Paul Praise Program," with the portraits of Silas and myself on the front. . . .

CORNY (*interrupting*): I didn't know you had that much hair, Paul.

PAUL (*laughing*): Thanks, Corny. Thanks a lot! I'll get you for that. (*Cut to Corny, laughing, then back to Paul.*) And on the back the words "World Tour IV—62 A.D.," with a map of the Mediterranean. Please send your love gift today. T-shirt supplies are limited. (*Turns, places T-shirt behind couch; faces stage right.*) Hey, let's have a song! SAPPP Singers, are you ready to bless us? Corny, take it away!

(*A technician hits the accompaniment track, and suddenly the studio is suffused with violins and trumpets. The SAPPP Singers, positioned on boulders in the fake stream and lake belt out an upbeat number— "Rock Me Gently"—their movements perfectly scripted, their smiles effusive, their arms spreading and raising as one in a crescendo of power on the last climactic note. Applause thunders from the audience. The SAPPP Singers bow with putative humility. Cut to Paul standing at couch, sniffing, mopping cheeks.)*

PAUL: They always do that to me. Thank you, SAPPP Singers. Let's hear it for the SAPPP Singers! (*Applause rocks studio; Paul composes self, turns to Silas.*) I never really know how to introduce our first guest, Si. Author, evangelist, pillar of the church, practitioner of exemplary piety? He's done it all. (*Turns to audience and begins shouting.*) Let's give a great big praise welcome to . . . James the Just!

(Paul and Silas clap hands enthusiastically while turning toward ramp, stage left. James trots down ramp to the couches, hugs Paul, then hugs Silas. All three sit on couches, Paul and Silas on left, James on right.)

PAUL *(leaning over, grabbing James' hand)*: Always exciting to see you, Jim. Where have you been? What have you been doing? What ga-a-a-reat things have been happening in your life?

JAMES *(intently)*: Well, . . .

SILAS *(interrupting)*: I hear you're coming out with a letter soon.

JAMES: Yes, Si, I've finished the manuscript and it's at the calligrapher's now.

PAUL: What're you going to call it?

JAMES: We're having a problem with that. My calligrapher wants to go with *The Epistle of James*. But I want *Your Formula for Holy, Practical Living*, or something catchy like that.

PAUL: You know, a title means so much. I battled many long hours with my calligrapher, too, over *The Epistle to the Galatians*.

SILAS: Now there's a title with some zip! *(All laugh.)*

PAUL: I can't help thinking a better title might have boosted sales. I wanted *Grace Through Faith—The Road to Salvation*, but . . .

JAMES *(interrupting)*: Sounds heavy—not too practical.

PAUL: Well, it *is* heavy.

JAMES: And you wonder why sales are sluggish, you old tentmaker? *(Forced laughs.)* Practicality, my man. Lifestyle. Applied daily living. You've got to figure, Paul, what are they going to be talking about two thousand years from now? This stuffy old heavy doctrine, or lifestyle Christianity?

PAUL *(looking quickly to wing, left)*: Oh, we have to take a break? Let me do this. *(Extreme close-up.)* Folks, as you know, we are gearing up for that big trip to Spain, and as Si mentioned earlier *(extreme extreme close-up)*, we . . . need . . . your . . . help. The T-shirts are fine. We've got lots of them for our love partners, but we have something else too. *(Camera falls back; Paul leans over side of couch and pulls out a vial of dust which he shows the audience.)* For our special love partners who send us a love gift of two hundred denarii we will send you . . .

(Suddenly, all lights go out, throwing studio into darkness. Some people scream. Technicians scurry about, attempting to fix the problem. One techie races to Paul with a lighted candle, which Paul takes in hand and stalks to the on-camera, holding his face, slightly illuminated from the candle, inches from the lens.)

PAUL *(into camera)*: I command you, Satan, begone from the power system. Depart from the electrical circuits of this studio, turn it back over to the Lord this second. I command you: Do it! Now!

(Suddenly, lights go back on. Silas and James throw up their arms and shout "Hallelujah!" and "Praise the Lord!" The audience screams its approval. Paul throws fists into air, shouts "Yes!" and prances back to his couch.)

PAUL: The Devil would like to see this television ministry go down the tubes, friends. That old Devil wants this show *off the air!* But are we gonna let it happen? *(Looks at James and Silas, who vigorously shake heads no.)* No way, Jose! We're going to whip that Devil! That old Devil doesn't have a snowball's chance in hell to put *us* off the air. *(To Silas.)* Now, where were we?
SILAS: Love gifts—two hundred denarii.
PAUL: Oh yeah. Right. *(Extreme close-up.)* But we need your love gifts, folks. That old Devil is in Spain, too. He doesn't want us to go. And you can help beat back Satan. For every love gift of two hundred denarii we will send you this *(holds vial to camera)* . . . this *(looks at vial, furrows brow, turns to Silas imploringly)* . . . this . . .
SILAS: Vial of dust from Pisidian Antioch.
PAUL: Right. A vial of the very dust Barnabas and I shook from our feet after sticking it to those agents of Satan in Pisidian Antioch. *(Paul puts vial on table, turns to side, picks up cellophane bag and shows it to camera.)* And for a love gift of five hundred denarii or more, we will send you this very special love gift—we have a *very* limited supply—a package of the actual scales that fell from my eyes in Damascus when Ananias put his hands on me.

(A "Holy Scribbler" runs onto stage bearing several scrolls. He hands them to Paul and trots off.)

PAUL: It's letter time, folks. Do we get letters! *(Breaks wax on one scroll, unrolls it, looks at bottom, begins to read.)* This is from Natty in Neapolis. "Dear Apostle Paul," Natty writes. "Before I watched your show the third lumbar vertebra in my back was hurting me big-time. My unbelieving husband said it was because I balanced the jugs of water I carry from the city well on my head wrong, but I knew it was something else. He made me a yoke to wear around my neck so I could balance two jugs on either side, but that didn't help. My third lumbar vertebra was killing me. Then one night when my husband was out getting rowdy down at the docks, I tuned in your show. And, Mr. Paul, that night you healed my back. I just want to thank you for blessing me." *(Paul looks tearfully into camera.)* Signed, "Natty from Neapolis."

SILAS *(effusively)*: Pa-a-a-raise the Lord!

PAUL: You know, Si, I remember that program. I remember feeling that somebody out there had a problem—I didn't see it clearly—it was a back or a neck or a leg or an arm—but it was clear *something* was hurting *somebody somewhere.* And that that person lived in Neapolis, or Amphipolis, or . . . or . . .

SILAS: Minneapolis?

PAUL: Right. Someplace with a "polis" in it. But how wonderful! How great! *(To camera.)* It blesses us to know that we bless you, folks. Send us those letters. *(Rolls scroll up, puts it beside couch.)* And now, a very special guest. A man whose ministry is just taking off. Best-selling author with a new autobiography just off the scribes' tables. Host of his own ever-popular television show and guest host here on S-A-P-P-P. Give a big praise welcome to . . . Timothy!

(Paul, Silas, and James stand and turn to ramp right, clapping enthusiastically. Timothy prances down ramp, arms uplifted, to the couches, where he embraces Paul, Silas, and James, who moves to the end of the couch farthest from Paul. Timothy sits on couch where James had been.)

PAUL: Tim, as always, a wonderful privilege to have you on. How's the ministry?

TIMOTHY (*gushing*): Incredible! Unbelievable! Awesome! Super! Amazing! Stupendous!

SILAS: Going pretty good, eh, Tim?

TIMOTHY: Oh man, fabulous! Tremendous! Great! Marvelous! Absotivelyposolutely super!

PAUL: You know, Tim, I hear about your self-esteem seminars wherever I go. Thessalonica, Troas, Corinth. People are really charged up about it.

TIMOTHY: Have you got that right, brother! The "Exorcizing Timidity with Timothy" seminars are going great guns. We are changing lives, brother! From timid, tired, sniveling, wimpy Christians to bold, authoritative, high self-esteem leaders. We're making it happen all over Macedonia. And this summer we're moving into Asia Minor. (*Into camera.*) For all you believers in the Lystra-Iconium area, mark the weekend of July 5 and 6 on your calendar. We'll be there. We'll be doing the show live. On the twelfth and thirteenth we'll be in Perga, and on the nineteenth and twentieth a big "Self-esteem Jamboree" direct from the amphitheater in Ephesus.

PAUL (*shaking head in wonder*): You know, Tim, I remember you back in the old days, a young man lacking self-assurance, a diffident little pipsqueak who was afraid even to appear on my show, much less host a show of his own. And now this widespread and famous ministry, with seminars and TV shows and Christian cruises. It's awesome to see the Lord working in your ministry, Tim.

TIMOTHY: I'm glad you brought up the cruise, Paul—another area the Lord is blessing us. (*Into camera.*) In August, folks, we'll be setting sail on our third annual "*Agape* Boat" cruise to Crete, Malta, Cyprus, and Sicily. Fun, games, fellowship, swimming, fishing, dancing at night to the SAPPP Singers, daily sessions in self-esteem teaching. Everyone who goes on the "*Agape* Boat" comes back a new creature. And surprisingly, we still have a few openings for the August cruise. To reserve a place write to (*address flashes on screen*) "Timothy, Thessalonica 4303." That's "Timothy, Thessalonica

4303." It'll get there. I've got my own zip code. But you must act quickly. Only a few openings remaining.

PAUL (*looking to wing left*): Tim, can you come back tomorrow?

TIMOTHY: Of course, brother. I can be here.

PAUL: Good. Because, unfortunately, we're out of time. The hour goes so quickly. And we haven't even talked about your new autobiography. (*Theme song begins as Paul looks directly into camera.*) Join us tomorrow, folks. Timothy will be here again. And Gaius and Aristarchus will be here, too, and of course, the SAPPP Singers to bless us with song. But whatever you do, wherever you go, remember . . .

ANNOUNCER: God wants that thorn to be shorn!

(*Camera falls back as theme song grows louder. Paul, Silas, James, and Timothy stand, shake hands, hug each other. The SAPPP Singers move over to the couches, exchange embraces, mill about, put hands in air, wiggle fingers, clap hands, sway in unison.*)

ANNOUNCER: For more information about how you can become prayer partners of the "Silas and Paul Praise Program," write Paul, c/o House Arrest, Convict No. 3765842, Rome 0017. That's Paul, c/o House Arrest, Convict No. 3765842, Rome 0017. And until next time, this is the "Silas and Paul Praise Pro-o-ogram-m-m!"

Cantor Yo-Hahn and the
Minister of Music

Minister of Music Elray Schlockmeister threw his swivel chair back and cupped his face in his hands. *How long, O Lord? How long?* he thought. Run an ad for an assistant minister of music in a couple of periodicals and you never know what will turn up. He expected everything from little old white-haired ladies who could make their electronics bleed syrup when they played "Blessed Assurance" to soi-disant garage-band wanna-bes with hard-driving, gut-level lyrics looking to springboard onto the Stryper tour. But this—the living and breathing anachronism seated a few yards away—this chapped his heinie. Who was screening these application forms, anyway?

"Tell me, Yo-Hahn," Schlockmeister said, attempting to mask his irritation. "How would you describe your sound?"

"Sound, sir?" replied the elderly, bewigged candidate.

Schlockmeister threw his head back and glared at the ceiling.

"Yeah, sound," he said. "Bag. You know, like DeGarmo and Key are like the Doobies; Petra is like Journey; Phil Driscoll is like Joe Cocker; Reba Rambo is like Crystal Gayle. You know, where do you fit in?"

"Well," said the other, "my primary métier is polyphonic, contrapuntal concerted music. Motets, cantatas, oratorios. But I also love the organ—organ partitas, preludes, toccatas, and fugues. I'm known for my mastery of figured bass. Pedals, you know. And I love the chorale. And I guess I have been influenced by Italian opera."

Elray Schlockmeister was tapping his pen on his teeth. "The 'Praise Strings' sort of sound is not big these days, Yo-Hahn," he said.

"I beg your pardon."

"Violins, oboes, flutes—that sort of thing? Not a whole lot of demand." He paused. "But when you come right down to it, performance is really a secondary consideration for this job. . . ."

"I play many instruments."

"Hmm. . . . But as I was saying, it's secondary. We want somebody who can play music, sure. And one more musician helps out, true. But really now, here at First Fruits we are blessed with scads of artists. We pride ourselves on our musical outreach. I think you'll find the music here top-drawer. Our praise and worship team—the Holy Hands (they lead about half the worship services)—is top-of-the-line. Did the Crouch show last month. And when we want something a little more with-it, we have the Living Stones. You're familiar with their work, of course."

"Forgive me, sir, I am not."

Schlockmeister shook his head in dismay. "You haven't heard of the Living Stones?" A look of profound incomprehension spread across the old burgher's face. "'(I Can't Get No) Sanctification' received a Dove nomination last year. They do everything from hearts-and-flowers to anointed torch to techno-pop to heavy metal. Very versatile.

"Then there are the Holy Rappers—at the cutting edge of the genre. And, of course, the Seven Vials. They nearly invented eschato-rock. Very hard stuff. Makes Rez Band sound like the World Action Singers. We press our own vinyl in-house for them—the Horse Bridle High label. Plus I have dozens of solo artists willing to sell their souls to get onto our platform." Schlockmeister hoisted a sheaf of papers from his in-basket as documentation.

"No, Yo-Hahn, performance is not key."

The cantor looked up from his hands, his lips pursed into a round mound of skepticism.

"What I'm looking for"—Schlockmeister brought his hands over his head and began encircling an imaginary globe three feet in diameter in the air—"is somebody who can pull it all together. Plan worship. Pick the songs. Rehearse the band. Find competent substitutes when our boys are on tour. Somebody with good musical taste who also has a gift for organization."

"This, sir, I have been doing my entire career," Yo-Hahn said. "If you will look at my résumé, you will see that my experience as both kapellmeister and cantor commends me for the position. At Leipzig I coordinated the music every Sunday for five churches. Including weekday services, I oversaw the music for twenty-two services."

"I see." Elray Schlockmeister pulled a thick manila folder onto his lap, threw open the cover, and began leafing through a stack of papers. "And, of course," he said, his eyes on the papers, "part of the job is to do a little composing. You know, something of your own."

"For the festivals of the church year?" said the musician. "Yes, of course. Some of our festivals ran three days in length. I regularly composed special music for those. Much of which, if I may say so, was of exceptional quality."

Schlockmeister waved two thick scores in the old fellow's face. "That's what these are, I suppose."

Yo-Hahn looked at them. "The 'Magnificat in D.' Yes. And the *Mass in B Minor.* Yes, sir. Samples of special music I have written."

Schlockmeister looked up. "You have anything for Pack-a-Pew Sunday?"

"Uh, no, sir," Yo-Hahn replied.

"How about Parking Lot Attendant Appreciation Sunday? That's a church festival here. You have anything for that?"

"I do not, sir."

"I see." Schlockmeister laid the scores on his desk and looked abstractedly at the wall. *A guy like this makes the short list? Unbelievable!* He leaned forward with an air of resignation. Might as well get it over with. "Let me tell you what we're going to do here, Yo-Hahn. I want you to go to your hotel room tonight, work up music for a service—you know, pick songs, arrange a little presermon mood music. Treat it like a regular Sunday worship service. Just the sort of thing you would do if you already had the job. Then tomorrow you come in, rehearse the band, work a little with the solo artist. That way I can observe your style, see how you perform under actual working conditions. And meanwhile I'll have a chance to look over this stuff"—he waved the manila folder—"and we'll get together on Thursday for another little session. Okay?" Schlockmeister stood abruptly and thrust his hand across the desk.

Yo-Hahn remained seated. "Uh, sir?" he said.

"What is it?"

"I assume you will be using the assigned propers for the day?"

Schlockmeister stared at him uncomprehendingly. "Huh?"

"The Epistle and the Gospel—the assigned pericopes for the Fourteenth Sunday after Pentecost. I assume I am to base my music on the readings."

"Oh, no no no," Schlockmeister said. "We don't do any of that stuff."

Yo-Hahn made an imploring gesture with his hands. "Well, how about the sermon? That will be based on the Gospel, of course?"

"Let me see." Schlockmeister sat back down. He plunged into a drawer in his desk and extricated a manila folder from which he pulled a sheet of paper. "Here we go," he said. "I can give you the sermon title. Maybe that will help some."

Yo-Hahn nodded once in decorous assent while Schlockmeister scribbled on a scrap of paper, folded it, and handed it to the bewigged German, who received it with a bow before unfolding it and reading its contents.

He leveled his eyes at the minister of music. "Thank you, sir. This will be a challenge."

The paper read, "You Can't Give It If You Ain't Got It: Ten Principles of Christian Money Management."

"Well, Yo-Hahn, I've got some bad news and some good news."
Elray Schlockmeister ran his hand across his face. His mind raced to
his next interview as he readied himself to dismiss this antediluvian
no-hoper. "Perhaps," he said, "you are aware of the bad news?"

Yo-Hahn's mind searched the recent past. "Ah, yes," he said.
"Yesterday's rehearsal."

"An interesting approach, to say the least," Schlockmeister said.
He scratched his Adam's apple. "And while I appreciate your creative efforts, it really did not go down well with the musicians. The
sword didn't help, either." Yo-Hahn bowed his head. "And then
continually referring to the musicians as Zap . . . er, Zimp, er . . . "

"*Zippelfagottist,* sir. Nanny-goat bassoonists."

"Right. That did not lend an edifying spirit to the proceedings.
The Living Stones didn't appreciate that. Constantly shouting 'pia-
nissimo' at our guitarists surely didn't help. What do you want, guy?
They had their amps at one-and-a-half! And as for the Holy
Hands—they really couldn't get into that song you selected for
them."

"*Wir glauben all an einem Gott.*"

"Was that it? . . . Not a very user-friendly song, in my opinion."

"The Creed, sir. Every proper service has the Creed in some
form. It gives the people a connection with the past to know that
their forebears from nineteen centuries have voiced the same faith,
the one true, holy, catholic, apostolic faith. It's the historic church's
response to Jesus' question, 'Who do you say I am?'"

"Well, our people are connected with the present here. . . . And
besides, that tune won't sing, Yo-Hahn. At least not here. The Holy
Hands are versatile, true. Classics like 'I Exalt Thee,' 'Thou Art Worthy,' and 'His Name Is Wonderful' for slow stuff, and more rock-
oriented tunes to whip up the spirit, but this '*Veer globben*' stuff? No
way! Our people know what they like, and they like rock-oriented,
subjective songs."

"On the contrary, sir, they like what they know. Were you to teach them the historically accepted liturgy with enthusiasm, they would like that," Yo-Hahn said.

Schlockmeister snorted and shook his head. "Well, anyhow, there was that. And then, the way you handled the soloist." Schlockmeister sighed. "Shall we put it diplomatically and say you lacked tact?"

"I allowed her to sing her song, sir." Yo-Hahn's face was all solemnity. "That was a major concession on my part."

"That was an original composition, by the way. 'Swell Was My Heart When My Heart Swelled.'"

"I merely asked her to quit that . . . *bleating.* She had no conception of rhythm; she slid into every other note; she had a vibrato that could bring down a cathedral; in short, she carried on like a *diva.* Such gushing I have never heard before. I merely asked her to let the song do the work, sir."

"LaVita LaSchmalz was second runner-up for the *Charisma* magazine Readers' Choice award last year, I'll have you know. Unemployed assistant ministers of music do *not* tell LaVita LaSchmalz how to sing!" Yo-Hahn grunted. "And then there was this." Schlockmeister tossed a thick score onto his desk.

"Ah yes, the cantata," Yo-Hahn said.

"Where did you come up with this thing?"

"The libretto is taken from biblical and hymnic sources. I wrote it as an *explicatio textus,* a musical sermon intended to produce repentance and faith. A proclamation of law and gospel. That's how I choose all of the music for worship. . . . I will admit, however, that the sermon title you supplied did give me some pause."

"I can see that. 'They that will be rich fall into temptation and a snare'?"

"First Timothy six-nine, sir."

"That won't fly here, Yo-Hahn." The minister softened his tone. "This idea of singing Scripture, though, we do that here, too, with our Scripture choruses." Yo-Hahn's face brightened. "The same verse over and over, sometimes for ten or fifteen minutes."

Then it darkened again. "For what purpose?" Yo-Hahn asked.

"The key is emotional content, Yo-Hahn. The same chorus repeated over a period of time produces the feelings we want in our people. The happy glow, the warm heart. The ever-building melody, the repetition—it works on the heart."

The German turned sardonic. "Perhaps someone should introduce you to the power of words, sir," he said. But the thrust was parried.

"This music of yours is also emotional," Schlockmeister said, hefting the cantata. "At least, theoretically."

"But with a difference, sir. It doesn't stress feeling and solemnity. The singer is not the subject of the lyrics. It stands in employment of the Word and exposition of Scripture, and it tells the gospel story. A couple of my major works—the *Passions*—do this more explicitly. I believe I supplied one in my folder."

Schlockmeister flipped through the scores on his desk. "You mean this?" he asked, waving *The Passion According to St. Matthew.* "Interesting. Sort of an early *Godspell,* eh?"

Yo-Hahn's face went blank.

A silence ensued.

"You spoke of some good news also, sir?"

"Good news? Oh yeah. Good news." Schlockmeister leaned back in his chair. Now he was all conciliation. "Obviously, Yo-Hahn, you have some talent. The cantatas, the *Passions,* this 'Magnificat' thing. Anybody who even tackles such ambitious projects must have something on the ball. I ran this one by Perry the other night." Schlockmeister pointed to a score on his desk. "He works the mixing board, and he seemed to think it had some possibilities. So I got the boys to bang out a few measures. Listen to this."

Schlockmeister punched "play" on his office boom box. It was the Gloria from the *Mass in B Minor* for four guitars and a synthesizer pumped up to head-banger wattage. Yo-Hahn fell out of his chair.

"Yeah! It blew me away too. Awesome!" Schlockmeister's voice pierced the din. "Catch this bass riff, Yo-Hahn. Anointed! Anointed!"

Schlockmeister hit the "stop" button. His voice returned to normal. "But anyway, we'd like to buy the rights to this piece and market it as a 'believercize' track—you know, Christian aerobics. . . . What is it again?" He shuffled through the scores as Yo-Hahn picked himself up off the floor. "This, uh, *Mass in B Minor.* As it's written here we can't use it. But with a little work—hey, how does *Shake Those Masses* grab you?—I think we could make it a hit. Wha'd'ya say?"

Yo-Hahn was standing at the desk. "Sir," he said, his voice tremulous. "I have nothing to say."

Schlockmeister skirted the desk and put a hand on the old man's shoulder. "Don't worry, Yo-Hahn, we'll cut you in on the royalties."

Yo-Hahn looked him straight in the eyes and said evenly, "Good day, sir."

"Okay," Schlockmeister said. "But think about it. I'll get back to you. We'll do lunch." Yo-Hahn turned to leave.

"And before you go"—Schlockmeister turned and shuffled more papers on his desk—"Ah, here it is. Maybe you could tell me something. There's a guy coming in this afternoon. Also a candidate for the post. He sent a picture, and I couldn't help but notice the resemblance. Same sort of outfit. A wig. Everything." He showed Yo-Hahn the picture. "Goes by Georgy Fred Handel. Sounds country. But he sure don't look country."

"I know of him, sir," Yo-Hahn said. "We both applied for a job in Lübeck."

"Oh?"

"Buxtehude's job. We both turned it down."

Some cheek, Schlockmeister thought. *This guy turning down a job.*

"As long as you don't have an ugly daughter, he might be your man," Yo-Hahn said, pulling the door closed.

"Huh?" Schlockmeister raced to the door, popped his head into the hallway, and called after the departing cantor. "Think about what I said. We'll make it worth your while."

Church Growth

Tips from the Experts

Church Growth That Works:
Breaking the Shackles of Tradition

It was something that I, in my short but ecclesiastically active span in this world, had never seen before. Sitting in the pew in front of me was a couple who had unsheathed two magazines from a traveling case at their feet and had begun to read them simultaneously with the beginning of the homily. One cradled in his hands an edition of *One World,* the World Council of Churches' official organ, while his partner flipped through the pages of *The Nation.* Given the leftist socio-political bent of the sermon emanating from the chancel, I, had I been more prescient, would surely have armed myself for counterattack. But I don't normally bring *National Review* to church.

So I was left to ponder the significance of the scene. I mulled over the unconscionable hubris exhibited by these brazen clucks in reading magazines during worship for a while before I was thunderstruck with the possibilities that their behavior contained. This had church growth potential! And while it was unlikely that this particular congregation was viewing the world through "church growth eyes," that fact did not negate the utility of the concept.

Magazine racks in the narthex, newspaper vendors hawking Sunday editions outside the doors, perhaps even best-sellers in the pew racks—these practices could go far in luring people into the sanctuary. They comply nicely with the precept that worship is to be made attractive. A pastor must make people want to attend his church. Thus we see church growth doctrines manifest themselves in particular actions: sanctuary and parking lot space must be ample, the worship service must be a high-quality celebration, visitors must be accorded lavish mid-service treatment, etc.

Yet there has been a tragic paucity of new ideas lately. The measures in current use are all tried and true; some have been with us since the movement's genesis back in the 1950s. But where are the new ideas? What are the visionaries envisioning? It seems that nobody is thinking up anything new that works anymore.

Magazines work. How many of the hard-core unspiritual could be drawn into the sanctuary were it broadcast that their favorite periodical (within limits) was available in the pew racks? Small televisions with VCR capability would work even better. The truly visionary pastor could construct a cassette display right next to the tract rack. Yet who is thinking about these sorts of things?

I am! And I herewith offer a primer of new strategies guaranteed to meet people where they are, to speak to people's needs and thus present an even more attractive ecclesiastical package:

1. *Beyond Greeters.* It has been twenty years or so since greeters descended in a meteor shower of amicability into our dreary narthexes. But after two decades, the time has come for this revered church growth custom to be subjected to our hard pragmatic eyes.

Remember the enthusiasm with which we embraced the concept? How ingenious it seemed to run worshipers through a gauntlet of well-wishers with eyes asparkle and sinewy handshakes that could force farmers onto their knees? It was such a master stroke—an epiphany—to realize that the organized church must present an overtly friendly mien. Greeters said something to the outside world. They communicated.

Now, of course, greeters are ubiquitous. Even Wisconsin Synod Lutherans have them. Thus the question must be broached: Do they work? Has their happy presence transformed our heretofore dour communions into bubbling founts of Christian cheer? The answer is no. Many churches—even some subscribing to church growth methodology—remain sepulchral tombs of Christian gloom. Greeters just don't get the job done anymore. People are onto them. They don't work.

More intense strategies of enforced friendliness are required. To this end, I suggest the concept of smilers. Beyond the phalanx of greeters, we must establish teams of smilers, groups of a dozen or so members designated to stand about the narthex, to walk to and fro, to be about normal Sunday morning business, but with the proviso that huge Jimmy Carter grins be carved onto their faces. Congregations truly serious about church growth could stipulate that the narthex be a Smiling Zone. "The Mile of Smiles." Or, in a more progressive vein, it could unilaterally be declared a "Frown-Free Zone." The time has come to move beyond greeters.

2. *Measuring the "Love Quotient."* Name tags are important. In churches with multiple services they are critical. For how is the 8:30 A.M. crowd to know if a non-name-tag wearer is truly a visitor or merely one of the eleven o'clock gang who got up early one Sunday? Embarrassing questions occasionally ensue, offense is sometimes taken, and the net minus is that parishioners grow less willing to engage non-name-tag wearers in any conversation whatever for fear of offending some tagless person who also happens to be a charter member of the congregation. Thus undeserved, a church can gain a reputation for chilliness.

Name tags are *de rigueur* in church growth churches. All agree. Yet church growth research has been strangely silent on this crucial front. What of these name tags? What type is best? How big should they be? How stylish? What if some clothes-horse in your congregation balks at pinning a giant green circle that proclaims "HI! I'M WILBUR" onto his six-hundred-dollar suit? Do happy faces work? Lots of questions. No answers.

As a private endeavor, I conducted some research recently and arrived at some rather useful conclusions about name tags. In visiting a dozen churches of varying denominations, I found a direct correlation between the size of the name tag worn and the friendliness exhibited by the individuals wearing them. Parishioners in stuffy and incongenial churches wore tiny, barely visible, nondescript printed tags, while those in parishes that nearly crackled with bonhomie donned tags the size of small pizzas. Those who adorned their tags with personal art work were the chummiest of all. Happy-face buttons, incidentally, seemed to bear no linkage whatever with the affability of the wearer.

3. *Feelings Quantification.* Is the movement behind the curve in technology? It's a valid question. Sure, computers have invaded growth churches nationwide, but they are called upon largely to perform mundane tasks like keeping attendance stats, classifying past growth data, and that sort of thing. What about engaging the issues of the heart?

We can preach all we want on the necessity of testing the soil, of gauging receptivity before actually dispersing the seed. And guidelines have been most helpful in quantifying a given recipient's or recipients' position on the continuum (see Engel, Holmes-Rahe, etc.). But all such quantification is purely subjective. How does one ascertain when another person is receptive? With the current thinking one looks at environment, sociology, and psychology—and then *guesses.* Mr. X just moved into the neighborhood—ergo, he's ripe. Miss Y just got fired—she's ripe. But sometimes Mr. X and Miss Y are *not* ripe.

What has technology done for us lately in this crucial growth area? Scarce little, unfortunately. That's why I feel it a distinct privilege to be able to unveil a revolutionary new invention that can take the guesswork out of receptivity.

The feel-o-meter. For the needs-meeting ministry, nothing can top it. Here's how it works: Parishioners hook up one tiny electrode to their fingertips. Their emotions as they listen to the sermon and sing the songs are recorded by a team of technicians in the church office, and the readings are transmitted to the pastor (pulpit fax machines are helpful here). That way the pastor always knows if he's meeting the people's needs and can adjust his sermon at any time.

The feel-o-meter also comes in handy during praise singing. In emotional services the pastor never really knows when his people's hearts have been sufficiently warmed to hear the gospel. Sure, after thirty-five minutes of repeatedly singing the same song one would *think* the people were ready. But who knows for sure?

I'll never forget how this truth was brought home to me. As a public service to church growth pastors everywhere, I recently set out on a fact-finding mission, visiting growing churches around my city to see why and how they were growing. One large church I visited made use of praise singing prior to the sermon. On the Sunday I attended, the singing began somewhat slowly and nonemotionally, with the congregation feeling its way through the rhythm and words. We were clearly just getting warmed up. After a few repeats, the songleader started waving his arms a little more fervently; the three soloists standing in front of the eighty-member choir started trading off solos. After about twenty minutes the brass section of the orchestra stood and picked up the pace. Five minutes later the orchestra as a whole stood and started to sway. And all the while the volume in the sanctuary kept building and building as if the song were a sort of spiritual "Bolero." My seat was shaking like a "Sensaround" theater seat.

Wow! I thought. *This place is rocking!* Then I looked around at my fellow parishioners, and they were sitting in their seats like a bunch of Quakers—they seemed to be "centering down" or something. Very, *very* strange. Where was all the noise coming from? Only then did I notice it—each member of the eighty-member choir had a *personal hand-held microphone.* They appeared to be trying to swallow those things.

The noise level in that place was extremely deceptive. These people were clearly not ready to hear the message. Thirty minutes later when the pastor invited them up for a weeping session of recommitment at the railing, only a handful marched forward. Had this pastor been availed of the technology of the feel-o-meter, this ineffective presentation of the gospel could have been avoided.

Now, granted, some of the bugs still have to be worked out. But isn't this something the gurus of the movement should be working on?

4. *Everyone a Minister.* A great many breakthroughs in recent years have lifted up the laity vis-à-vis the intimidating presence of an

imperial clergy. Robes and vestments have been forsaken in some quarters; chancels and pulpits have been physically lowered; laity have been installed behind lectern and communion rail—all eroding the mighty barrier between clergy and laity and giving expression to the priesthood of all believers.

Yet the chasm remains. It is still the minister who preaches, baptizes, marries, and buries. The nimbus still hovers above those who walk piously about the chancels of our sanctuaries on Sunday mornings. They are somehow special, somehow different from everybody else. After all, who else intrudes into our lives with a twenty-minute monologue every week? Who else knows Greek? We in the pews still seem less involved, less important. And that makes us feel bad.

Thus my antidote: Make everyone a minister. Install everyone in special services. Put everyone's name on the masthead of the bulletin. Make everyone feel equally important. Sacralize everything. Transform the Sunday school superintendent into the minister of the Sunday school; install the trustees as ministers of the grounds and the server for the post-service fellowship hour as minister of the coffee grounds. Haul up the church-picnic helpers to the chancel and "ordain" them as such on the morning of the picnic.

This concept provides a solution to the committee-meeting problem as well. As all churches have committees, it is universally true that once established, these committees must meet. Thus we have meetings.

Nowhere on the ecclesiastical spectrum is this phenomenon more prevalent than in church growth churches. With each new program such a church undertakes, it establishes an attendant committee to oversee that program. I know from experience that in growing churches committees breed like rabbits. I have walked into committee meetings with the sole intention of overseeing the business of that particular committee, only to trudge out several hours later enlisted on the rolls of two or three additional ad hoc committees.

This would be fine, except for the fact that I—and I would warrant, church members in general—loathe meetings. For a variety of reasons, we hate them. Certainly every church lays claim to a band of inveterate meeting-goers, doughty souls whose adrenaline seems to flow at the mention of the real seven last words of the church: "Let's get together and meet on it." But this is a small minority of any church's membership, and newcomers especially are only frightened away if told they are expected to tramp on down to the church three nights a week.

What, then, can be done about the meeting problem? Why not go totally egalitarian and make everyone a committee? Churches filled with committees of one are much the case nowadays anyhow, so why not institutionalize them? There would be no competition for meeting space and no difficulty in finding a suitable meeting night. Congregational meetings might drag on a little with a super-abundance of committee reports, but that seems little payment for growth. I am continually amazed: Why has no one thought of these things before?

5. *Sermonic Aids.* The most crucial portion of any worship service is unquestionably the sermon. Here the pastor is accorded twenty minutes of relative quiet—twenty minutes during which the congregation can attend closely to his message.

However, some—albeit mostly parishioners—see this as a problem. Twenty minutes can be a long, long time. We came to recognize that early on. Thus a surfeit of sermonic alternatives has been spawned: chancel dramas, dialogue sermons, slide shows, laser-light extravaganzas, and the like. But these are not every-week options, and when a preacher offers traditional homiletic fare—as he certainly must—he often finds that he doesn't really capture his people's attention until he utters the curiously rehabilitative phrase "And in conclusion. . . ." And then it's too late. Sermons are still a problem.

Some continue to insist that the well-organized, theologically sound homily wrought by laborious hours of book work is an option. But please, let's talk reality here! People don't want that. They want a compendium of upbeat anecdotes and jokes culminating in a definitive list of how-tos.

So the problem remains: how to capture and retain the attention of a couple hundred parishioners, disparate in taste and widely varied in need. It is a dilemma that has haunted persons of the cloth since Luther's time, and even before. Luther, anyhow, had an advantage—

his congregation had to stand all the way through his sermons. Obviously we can't have that. We can't even get ours to stand for the reading of the gospel anymore. So we came up with the sermon outline instead.

Sermon outlines have served many uses; and great they are, too, so far as they go. But, here again, these aids have become predictable. Arranged in outline form with key words underlined or occasional spaces left blank for the parishioners to fill in, these outlines have become totally passé. A parishioner opening his worship folder to see the sermon outline thinks, "Here we go again; same old, same old"—and his mind is in full flight even before the preacher gets his opening joke out.

Give us an outline that holds our interest—acrostics or crosswords or mazes or connect-the-dots. Or even better, a critique sheet listing sermonic illustrations and jokes could be used, with a space before each to allow parishioners the chance to grade them. I cite as an example the following:

   B   Anecdote from my summer vacation

   B– Story about my first parish

   A+ Quality of straw man set up to portray member who is not in favor of church growth

   D   Theological relevance

   C– Gossip about man who came in for pastoral counseling

   A+ Joke about the nun and her horse-racing donkey

Worshipers will grade each item and deposit the outline in the offering plate—unsigned, of course. Thus the preacher's illustrations and jokes can be evaluated, parishioners have input, and future sermons can be written with the congregation's likes and dislikes in mind.

A few additional measures come to mind:

• Some avant-garde thinkers have suggested a high-speed aisle, much along the lines of moving airport walkways. This would provide parishioners wishing a quick and anonymous exit immediate transport from sanctuary to parking lot, thus evading the pastoral handshake and the narthex gabfest. This seems like a good idea.

• A pew-end seating section of the sanctuary. Pew ends are in much demand, as the percipient worshiper well knows. You've surely seen the solitary person who will plop down right on the end of a pew, cross his arms, and then refuse to move no matter how many others are forced to crawl over his legs to get to the middle. Or, surely you've seen how families will huddle at the end of a pew going through an Alphonse-and-Gaston routine to see who goes in first. Why not designate one area of the sanctuary as "Pew-End Seating Only"? Meet the people where they are—in this case, on the end of the pew.

• Also, the whole matter of ministry to the dehomogenized has never surfaced in mainstream church growth thinking. What of these forgotten victims of the early growth days who have been stamped as unhomogeneous members, accused of impossibility thinking, and stripped of all influence? The fact that the movement has envisioned no outreach here is troubling—and shortsighted.

Church growth was a movement possessed of some puissance in the early days, a revolution that changed habits and molded minds. Traditions were felled; a great body of sociological dogma grew up in their place; and now we have greeters, name tags, and preachers who will sell their confessional status for a stalagmite in their growth curve. But here, as always, the questions must be addressed: Does it still work? Does it carry the power it once did? Or is the revolution over? Have we entered the debilitating second stage, a period of retrenchment when the struggle against tradition has raised up for itself immutable traditions of its own?

We must rise to the challenge of breaking these shackles of church growth tradition, of dispelling the fog of success that has settled around our church growth eyes. We can't be satisfied with the past, with the status quo, with how things have always been done. We must always be thinking up new strategies that work.

And we can start with magazines.

How Unfriendly Toward Visitors Are You?

It's quiz time, folks. Just eight short, easy, multiple-choice questions geared to help you analyze one of the most important aspects of your church life. It's called, "How Unfriendly Toward Visitors Are You?"

I know it must sound odd to formulate a questionnaire with such an unconventional title—in the negative and all—but I think it important that we deal in fact and reality here. For that reason I do not title the questionnaire, "How Friendly Toward Visitors Are You?" because friendliness toward visitors, to be frank, is an anomaly in our churches. *Un*friendliness too often is the norm.

Now, don't get me wrong. Church people may be the most affable, congenial, loving, caring, self-effacing people on this earth, generally speaking. But when they are assembled in the narthex of their churches following Sunday worship, there is a wave of icy disaffection that breaks upon the shoals of their being. Strange faces, visitors, those outside their close coteries of acquaintanceship are shunned.

It's true! Why else would large assemblies of loving, caring Christians feel compelled to actually *appoint* people whose sole function at Sunday service is being friendly toward visitors? Why else would we commission phalanxes of greeters to stand with their right hands of fellowship outstretched at every church door?

I'll tell you why: Because if we didn't make people do it, it wouldn't get done.

We emphasize friendliness toward visitors in myriad ways: by pinning on special visitor name tags, by distributing visitor recognition packets, by having visitor introduction segments in our services, by signing guest registers, by having weekly exhortations from our pastors calling for geniality and love to be exchanged among all in attendance, but especially to the visitors.

Yet, despite all this, our churches remain bastions of gelid comportment. A visitor stands a better chance of male bonding with a member of the Supreme Soviet than he does of striking up a conversation in the church foyer following Sunday worship. I know. I visit plenty of churches, and the first thing I do when I walk out of most of them is smell my armpits.

One might even arrive at the conclusion that people *want* to be unfriendly toward visitors, that people are *happy* when they do not befriend visitors. Ergo, the tenor of the questionnaire.

But enough preamble. Let's do it. One answer for each question. No time limit. You'll be graded at the end.

1. You are sitting in a pew with your spouse and six children, the youngest of whom is two, and each of you has a hymnal and a worship folder of your very own. Next to your youngest, at the end of the pew, sits a visitor. He has no hymnal, no worship folder, and no idea whatsoever about what is going on. He looks lost, forlorn, befuddled. What do you do?
   a. Point out a different pew to him where there are some hymnals available.
   b. Tell him he can have the hymnal your two-year-old is crayoning in, but *he* has to take it away from the tyke.
   c. Give him your hymnal and guide him through the service.

2. When a visitor stands up to receive special recognition after the benediction, how do you greet that visitor?
   a. Boo him.
   b. Ask him to become Sunday school superintendent.
   c. Approach him after the service with words of welcome.

3. Visitors leaving your church after Sunday worship feel like
   a. Low-order invertebrates.
   b. Intruders at some invitation-only social gathering.
   c. Valued and loved members of God's creation.

4. As soon as the benediction and announcements have been completed and you have been dismissed by the pastor, you
   a. Blow out the doors as if somebody just blasted your rear end with a flamethrower.
   b. Hurry through the pastor's receiving line and then chum up to your friends to jaw about the latest gossip.
   c. Actively seek out any visitors and attempt to make them feel welcomed.

5. You are in the coffee line. You do not recognize the person in front of you, who is not wearing a name tag and has an expression on his face that is akin to that of the RCA Victor dog. He takes his cup of coffee and turns to look entreatingly toward you, hoping to strike up a conversation. What do you say?
   a. "Did you pay for that?"
   b. You say nothing, as you don't know if he's a visitor or not. Heck, you don't even know two-thirds of the members! And, besides, being friendly to visitors is the greeters' job.
   c. "Let me get you a guest name tag. Would you like to attend Bible class with me?"

6. Complete the following sentence: As far as a visitor is concerned, the chief difference between the lobby of my church following Sunday service and a busy New York City street at lunchtime on a working day is that
   a. On the New York City street some of the people might say, "Hi."
   b. On the New York City street they don't wear name tags.
   c. On the New York City street a person is not surrounded by Christian brothers and sisters who will go out of their way to make a visitor feel like an integral part of the Christian community.

7. The greeters at your church
   a. Are the grumpiest people in the entire congregation.
   b. Look at you in the greeting line as if you had just told them you shared the "Four Spiritual Laws" with Elvis the previous evening.
   c. Recognize the importance of presenting a positive first impression of the church.

8. What measure would be necessary to get the people at your church to befriend a visitor after Sunday worship?
   a. Dress the newcomer in a fluorescent orange hunting vest with the word "VISITOR" spelled out on front and back in five-inch-high letters and stand him in a roped-off area in the middle of the narthex during the fellowship hour.
   b. Issue him a garish visitor's name tag and drag him up to the front of the church after announcements for an embarrassing special introduction.
   c. Do nothing out of the ordinary, as people at your church naturally respond to a visitor with love and affection.

To tally your score give yourself ten points for every letter *a* you circled, five points for every letter *b*, and zero points for every letter *c*. Remember, we are attempting to determine how *un*friendly you are. Add your scores, then plug them into the following chart to find out where you stand on the unfriendliness index.

60–80   You are extremely unfriendly toward visitors. You won't have to worry about seeing *that* visitor again!

40–60   You are unfriendly toward newcomers. It will be a while before someone breaks into your post-service circle of conversation.

20–40   You are friendly toward visitors. Do others look at you quizzically?

0–20   You are extremely friendly. Look out! That visitor just might come back!

New Growth Community Center

(The Rev. Dr. Seymour Peeples has become a household name in church growth circles. Stepping into a seriously plateaued church, he breathed new life into a moribund congregation and established a ministry that is currently meeting the needs of thousands in the Midwest city of Zenith. But none of his fantastic growth came without a price. Dr. Peeples faced down adversity at every turn. He has become the world's leading authority on the theological aspects of the persistently faced and often debilitating pioneer-homesteader problem—dealing with the old guard, that rusty cadre of entrenched members found in every church that militates against change and growth. It is to help pastors facing similar challenges that we now allow Dr. Peeples to tell his story. This article is excerpted and adapted from his new book *O No Pioneers!*)

Pioneers. There is something about the word that sends church growth pastors into fits of anxiety. Entrenched in positions of power in the church, pioneers are like a wet blanket thrown onto the fires of growth, people out of all time and place, stubbornly resisting all progress, voting down crucial growth initiatives, poisoning debate with their obsession for retaining the status quo. Every growing church has them.

So, how does a growth pastor deal with them? Through love. Strong love. Tough love. Love that will stop at nothing. We know all too well the conventional tactics espoused to deal with these troublesome individuals. Greater men than I have laid down the strategems: don't attract them; don't feed them (they will seek "greener" pastures); don't give them a platform from which to spread their negativism (a growing church is *not* a democracy); allow strong laymen to confront them (no sense putting your own fanny on the block); never put them in a position of power; etc.

But the one aspect that has been largely overlooked in church growth literature is the pioneers' theological defense. Some of these folks present theological reasons—almost always erroneous—as justification for their opposition to growth. I think church growth pastors need to be aware of this line of thinking and of the viable arguments available to them when such challenges are broached. It is this particular facet of the pioneer-homesteader struggle that I wish to address in this chapter.

One of the first acts of our drama of growth here at New Growth was to change the name of the congregation. Reformation Lutheran Church—the old name—was obviously defective. And despite entrenched resistance—"A church name should indicate at the very least a definite place on the theological spectrum," one naysayer exclaimed—we settled on New Growth Community Center. We wanted a name that encapsulized our *raison d'être*—"New Growth"—and positioned our product within the prospective market. We also wanted to go nondenominational. "Find a Hurt and Heal It Christian Church" came in a close second. But such a name won't do. First, it is too long. Second, the words *Christian* and *Church* prove problematical. They carry too much negative freight in our society, erecting barriers that some people are simply unable to overcome.

Nondenominational status also allows the growth pastor to make an end run around the sticky question of doctrine. Because, face it, which doctrines are you going to preach about? Baptism? The Lord's Supper? Election and predestination? Eschatology? Not if you've got any church growth smarts, you won't. You draw people from a smorgasbord of denominational heritages—Catholic, Episcopalian, Hard-shell Baptist, Dunker, Nazarene, Pentecostal, Swedenborgian, and who knows what all else? Give some of these folks an opening, and they'll stage heresy trials.

Ironically, all this plays right into a nondenominational church's hands. For we who are truly committed to growth are left to offer the only thing people want: lifestyle Christianity. In theological terms—sanctification. Americans want results; they're interested in action, not ideas, in the practical, not the theoretical. I preach *nothing* but how-to sermons—how to love, how to be patient, how to overcome fear, how to beat loneliness, how to handle money, how to practice encouragement. My research teams gather data on the areas of community hurt, and I address them. And we've just expanded from four to six Sunday services. Clearly, we are healing the hurting.

We concluded that the optimal method for growth is to meet people's needs. And straightaway the marketing paradigm took hold. Nowhere was this more explicit than during our executive board's decision to adopt a church motto. How to speak to the community in a way that captures our spirit, our vision, our availability, our friendly accepting attitude. And do it in one phrase. It is a problem that haunts everybody from IBM to Marlin's Plumbing, and we wanted to get it right. In the end, my suggestion stuck—"New Growth Community Center: It just feels right"—although discussion ran hot and heavy (and frequently negative) at more than a few board meetings. Not too specific, not too informational, just enough of a hook to draw hurting people with needs through our doors. And it sure beats some of the other suggestions: "Don't do drugs, do Jesus at New Growth Community Center" (too flip); "At New Growth the quality goes in before the name goes on" (untrue); and "New Growth: A church of creedal, confessional, liturgical, sacramental integrity" (blatantly untrue).

Not even these elementary measures escaped virulent opposition, however.

Speaking at an executive board meeting three months into my tenure, one man, August Silage by name, sounded his first public sour note. "It seems to me," Silage said, "that in many ways this obsession with lifestyle Christianity is nothing but a capitulation to the American zeitgeist. You are coddling to experience, pastor. In addition to the theological ramifications—that is, the heretical elevation of sanctification over and above justification—you, in your desire to heal people's hurts, have replaced objectivity with subjectivity. The objective gospel—the message of repentance and forgiveness—is in essence *very* practical. It is the message that renews the soul and allows Christians to go out and live Christian lives. You focus your theology on people, not that gospel; you define their needs by what they think they need, not by what God thinks they need. And thus experience becomes key.

"And furthermore," Silage continued, "it is just this sort of atomization that erodes the doctrine of the church. The church is corporate, pastor. We are the body of Christ. The concept of the church allows believers to lose themselves in a larger whole, which has a history. Your approach is individualistic. The only reason people come to this place is to have individual needs met. You are transforming this place into nothing but a glorified support group, where religious experience and personal piety unite, not the truths of historic Christianity, and I don't mind telling you that it bothers me."

Well, I don't mind telling *you* that it bothered *me,* too, at the time. This betrayal was unspeakably odious. Having one of my inner circle question the very cynosure of our philosophy. And in public to boot! It left me temporarily without retort and sent me scurrying to the works of the founding fathers, where I drank in the sweet and healing waters of . . . *research.* Studies show that doctrine does not build or unify churches. The estimable Paul Yonggi Cho says, "People are always coming to church in great need, but if the preacher is only talking about theology, history, and politics, the people are not going to be helped in their present lives where they need the message." And Cho's numbers speak for themselves. Cho knows growth.

Not that theology is not important. It is. But the way I read it, it's not *that* important. Baptist churches grow, and Lutheran churches grow. Expositional verse-by-verse sermons work in some churches, possibility-thinking sermons work in others. Name a theological position and I'll show you a growing church that espouses it. Church growth theology is local—use what works for you in your situation.

I remember another little excursus from the doughty old duffer. "It seems to me," the old rube said at another executive board meeting, "that doctrine is *more* important than practice. *Lex orandi, lex credendi.* What you believe has a direct relation to what you do, and if you're not highlighting your confession and affirming it over and over again, you'll lose your theological moorings. The affirmation of that faith is what strengthens that faith. Otherwise, you'll drift off into a sea of psychobabbling pish-posh, a whirlpool of misguided therapy that plays favorably with the masses, but pulls the linchpin from the entire enterprise."

Good old Silage. So much head knowledge, so little heart knowledge. *Doctrine does not build churches.* Sure, it's important, as long as it remains understood. And we never forget our theological antecedents here at New Growth. Why, we even highlight it in our church newsletter *twice a year.* A wall hanging directly above my desk spells out our theological nonnegotiables.

Note, however, that I didn't call it a creed. With creeds you run into another problem: A living, breathing faith, spontaneous and on fire, evolves into a lifeless formulation of dogma, which is then memorized and recited in zombie-like unison on Sunday mornings. People are turned off to creeds. Creeds smack of a forgotten time, a pre-Enlightenment age when things were much simpler. And I don't care if Silage, along with his ilk, says, "I am vivified in the knowledge that the same creed I speak on Sunday mornings was spoken by Augustine, by Athanasius, by Ambrose, by Aquinas, by Luther, by Calvin, by Melanchthon, and by Cranmer. It shows me that I'm confessing the faith of the ages. It gives me historical perspective. It tells me I'm part of the one holy, catholic, apostolic church. It imbues my faith with meaning."

Creeds. Doctrine. Church history. A meaningful linkage with the past. It's all long-gone and long-forgotten. My view of church history has some punch, some relevance, and it goes like this: First there was Moses, then there was Jesus, then there was Paul, and then there was Oral Roberts. That's where *I'm* coming from, and that's where the people I minister to are coming from.

Silage sang the same song on liturgy. My position on liturgy is "may it rest in peace." The idea of some pooh-bah in robes waltzing around an altar and offering up archaic and antiquarian incantations in some sing-songy voice and adhering to some arcane rubric because it had meaning for some peasants long ago in medieval Europe is total and unadulterated mumbo-jumbo. It stinks of establishment Christianity right down to the last smell and bell. The people don't want any of that stuff—it's totally alien to their experience. When I use liturgy—and on occasion I do—it had better be relevant and speak to today's world. That's why I make up my own.

"It seems to me," Silage said over the phone the Tuesday following one of the liturgies, "that history has never seen the equal to your arrogance, sir. To think that you can throw some pedestrian words together and deem it a suitable substitution for an order of service that has nurtured the body for fifteen hundred years is unbridled, unabashed, unameliorated arrogance. The historic liturgy recounts Good Friday and Easter; it produces and fosters repentance and faith; it gives all glory to Christ and ties our church with the church of Ambrose and Chrysostom and Luther and . . . "

"Yeah, yeah, I heard all that before, Auggie," I said, hanging up on him. Sometimes hanging up is the kindest thing a pastor can do. The particular liturgy the old coot got so worked up over happened to come together for me at five o'clock that Sunday morning in a booth at Denny's. I called it the "Grand Slam Liturgy." Favorable comments ran six to one afterward. I'll never forget the congregational enthusiasm, the lifting of ariatic voices, when we launched in unison into the hymn of praise:

> Growth is our calling;
> Of this we boast.
> The Devil is bawling;
> I want hash browns, not toast.

These pioneers were a bad dream I thought I would never wake up from. Normally a pastor blows into an old congregation, changes a few things, and following some disorganized resistance, the old-timers stomp away in a huff. I fully expected Silage and his crowd to do the same. After all, I'd messed with their treasured liturgy; I'd gone in for touchy-feely religion big time; I ignored them whenever I could; I didn't feed them with negative and ineffective sermons on doctrine or any other moribund topic. And they were hanging on like an oil slick.

It was then that I came up with the ultimate "love" solution. Because of the sensitivity of the measure, I cannot reveal it in this article. But suffice it to say, it is effective. Very effective. [See "The Church Growth Inferno," pages 159–72, for a look at this solution from a different point of view—Ed.]

Confronting pioneers is a task not to be taken lightly. Dealing with them in love is of course necessary. But sometimes the love has to get tough. Those rock-ribbed old-timers can sabotage God-ordained growth. As long as they're around, a pastor's growth curve will go nowhere but down.

Nineteen Tips for
Small-Group Survival

One of the most heralded outgrowths of church growth thinking in recent years has been the proliferation of small groups, also called cell groups. These groups, cut out of the local church and serving up to fifteen people, meet regularly in informal settings for Bible study, prayer, and sharing and are designed to build up the community of believers.

This is perfectly logical. You've got to figure, if a church is burgeoning, adding legions upon legions to its roles, the one thing that is bound to suffer in the process is community. If people had trouble putting names with faces when they had only 250 coming to church, think what a chore it would be with ten times that number.

Ergo, cell groups. That's where members get to know others. That's where they share, fellowship, lay out their problems, and connect with their fellows. That's where the real, meaningful personal interaction occurs.

It is nearly inconceivable for a growing church not to employ a small-group structure of some type. And although it is probably beyond the realm of possibility, there may be some out there on the American Christian scene who are still unfamiliar with these latter-day *collegia pietatis.* Some folks still wandering around in the catacombs of the past, equating Christian living with regular church and

Bible-class attendance, partaking of the Sacrament frequently, and reading their Bibles and praying at home, think cell-group structure must be something they missed in high school biology.

This chapter is for them. For, were they to be thrown unprepared into the cell-group scene at this stage in their lives, they very likely would not survive. The fact is, there are some behaviors that are *sui generis* to the cell-group concept—things like corporate-prayer protocol, the speaking of "evangelicalese," the ability to unabashedly reveal innermost thoughts and feelings. And if they can't adapt to these new behaviors, they'll be written off as unmalleable, inflexible, nonpliant evangelical stiffs.

Now, nobody's going to get too wired about that if they are, say, sixty-five-year-old rigid, formal, discipline-oriented Old World types for whom any show of emotion is regarded as weakness. Nobody, not even a cell-group leader, is going to expect them to instantly transmogrify into touchy-feely fountains of emotional power who get off on the fuzzy-wuzzy things of life.

But if they're under, say, forty and still come off like that, they're in big trouble. For to resist cell-group induction is to cast suspicion on their faith, as involvement in these conclaves is *de rigueur* for the discipled Christian.

Therefore, as a service to the tyro, we offer nineteen tips for cell-group survival.

1. Wear proper attire. Showing up for a cell group improperly attired can be fatal to your acceptance by the group. Wearing a three-piece suit with a shirt collar so starched that you have to turn your entire upper torso to look at somebody seated two chairs away while everybody else in the room is donning "The Righteous JUST DO IT by Faith" and "Beam Me Up JESUS" T-shirts can spell trouble. The watchword here is informality.

2. Never sit in the power chair. That's the group leader's place and is usually recognizable by the presence of fan-bearers at either side.

3. Sit on the same level with everybody else. Don't enter the room and immediately plop into a bean-bag chair unless everybody

else is sitting in a bean-bag chair. And don't perch yourself on a stool raised two feet higher than the people on the low-slung couch across the room who have to look up through the space between their knees just to see you.

4. Don't hide behind a lamp or large floral arrangement. The good host will remove these so nothing impedes the dynamics of sharing, but some hosts are, well, a little reluctant to rearrange their living rooms every time the cell group drops by. Help the hosts out by sitting in an acceptable spot. Also, don't sit opposite the television with the remote control in your lap, especially if the cell group meets on Monday nights during football season.

5. Don't sit in the middle of a couch. That way the people sitting on the ends don't have to lean out and talk around you to each other.

6. Sit properly. Don't slouch. Don't drape yourself over the chair like a pair of discarded pants. But don't sit ramrod-straight with your hands on your knees as if you had just been strapped into Old Sparky, either. Rather, sit on the edge of your seat in a posture of rapt attention, peering always into the speaker's eyes and nodding with affirmation at whatever he or she is saying.

7. Be ready for the icebreaker (also called "sharing") question. We say "be ready" rather than "be prepared" because nobody can really prepare for these things, as they are usually quite insipid. For example, "What is your favorite ice cream flavor and how do your feelings about it relate to your Christian walk?" These questions are designed to get you into a self-disclosing frame of mind so that you can share more effectively once the bona fide sharing begins.

8. Learn the lingo. If you're to be accepted in a cell group, you're going to have to speak the cell-group patois, also called "Christianese." This includes such enlightened phrases as "getting into the Word," "speaking to my heart," "lifting up to you, Lord," "laid upon my heart," "burden on my heart," "stepping out in faith," "trusting God to meet this or that need," "I feel led," "I feel under conviction," "fellowship" (used as a verb), and the incessant use of the word *just*, as in "We just thank and praise you, Lord." If you don't know these basics, you might as well not even show up.

9. Don't expect to learn anything. Cell groups are notoriously noncognitive. They are relational experiences, with heavy doses of sharing and pouring out your feelings and nodding sympathetically when your peers divulge their inner beings.

10. Don't talk too much. Do this, and the leader will put you in the chair next to him, as it is a proven psychological fact that the person sitting next to the leader keeps largely mute.

11. Don't talk too little, either. No sitting there spongelike in a posture of absorption. It depresses the rest of the group, and the leader will direct every other question to you personally to "draw you out."

12. Don't make a forceful authoritative statement early in the session and then attempt to hide under the cushions of your chair for the duration. The sanctification engineers will be on you in a second.

13. Be positive. No complaining, no criticizing, no negative comments about anything unless it's safe to be negative about a particular topic, like pornography or heavy-metal music or the New Age Movement. And, for heaven's sake, no arguing.

14. Don't discuss doctrine. Research shows that doctrine is a major turn-off. One of the reasons these folks are here in the first place is to get away from doctrine. To paraphrase the ecumenists, "Feelings unite, doctrines divide."

15. When someone says something of a heretical nature (as is commonplace), do not throw your head back and bay at the ceiling. And no snorting, harumphing, sneering, etc. Rather, thank that person for the opinion and then tell of someone you know at work who shares the same view.

16. Watch your body language. Cell-group leaders are trained to observe your every action and read into it volumes of unspoken truths. So don't fold your arms. Don't shake your head no every time somebody says something you don't agree with. And don't keep staring at the *objects d'art,* even if they are Elvis busts or blinking neon "Jesus Saves" signs.

17. You must pray out loud during the circle prayer. Oh sure, the only prayer you've ever said aloud outside the sanctuary has been the Lord's Prayer and the common table prayer, but that's no excuse.

You've got to relate. You can probably squeak by without saying anything for two meetings, three at the max. But eventually you must conform to the emotional regimen and vocalize your petition. One good primer prayer—to get your started—is, "Lord, I just ask you to lay on my heart a word to speak in this prayer here." But after that, you're on your own.

18. Always wipe your hands on your pants before joining hands for the circle prayer. Nothing is a bigger turn-off than fish hands in a circle prayer. Sure, you're sweating bullets; you're as uncomfortable with this thing as all get-out. But no sense displaying your discomposure to the entire group.

19. Be attentive to the tacit signals of corporate prayer. Don't open your eyes during long pauses. Be aware that a person who starts milking your hand as if it were a cow's udder wants to be skipped. And, by all means, don't automatically think the prayer is over if the person next to you suddenly breaks his or her grip. Check it out first. That person may only be "lifting holy hands." The prayer is not officially over until the leader delivers the wrap-up.

Happy sharing.

Ask the Consultant

Do we get letters! By the sackful. Pastors with growth problems, members with assimilation woes. And questions! People out there want answers to their church growth queries.

But, hey, that's what we're here for. We recently joined the ranks of the growing horde of church growth consultants—okay, our inclusion was a unilateral move (write a church growth book and you can be a consultant, too)—and we feel that our expertise can provide churches of all sizes with that extra little umph they need to turn those scars into stars and all that.

So, as a service to the many out there who are caught in the morass of nongrowth, we now respond to your many cards and letters with the straight poop—real, practical answers for today's growing church.

Q: What is church growth?

Just Curious in New York

A: Dear Just Curious,

Church growth is a body of empirically devised scientific principles based on sociology, anthropology, psychology, marketing, advertising, telecommunications, computer sciences, and the reading of goat entrails. And, oh yes, we toss a little theology in there just to keep the religious hardhats from raising too much of a stink.

Q: How can I tell if a pastor is really a church growth pastor?

Confused in Cicero

A: Dear Confused,

Good question. So much muddying of the waters has occurred in recent years that it is becoming ever more difficult to really tell if a pastor is the bona fide article. Some subscribe to the whole package—the homogeneous unit principle, the Receptivity-Resistance Axis, and everything else—and rightfully deserve the appellation "church growth pastor." Others stick a column of glad-handers at the church door and cut their grass every other day, and they call themselves church growth pastors, too, whereas in reality this second bunch is no more church growth than the pope. Everybody, it seems, wants to get in on a good thing. We thus further define the term by insisting that those wishing to be so labeled must buy the package pedaled by the church growth people in Pasadena, California.

Q: What *about* the pope? He seems to have pretty good church growth.

Seeking Clarification in Rome

A: Dear Seeking,

We don't count the pope. Nor do we count the 800 or 900 million people who follow the pope (although those numbers tempt us plenty). Although we strive to be overtly atheological, we have to draw the line somewhere. And infant baptism, all the hocus-pocus of the sacraments, and the incessant mumbo-jumbo of their liturgy is as good a place as any.

Q: First the facts: AGR—a measly 27.6 percent; DGR—an even worse 24.8 percent; AAGR—2.3 percent. Diagnosis: Nonterminal koinonitis caused by acute fellowship saturation. A-1 assimilation factors at play in the community with C-1 enculturation. Minimal E-0 type evangelism; absolutely no E-1, E-2, or E-3. I've got one op, two orgs, and zero cats. Problem of the 9.5 is really the problem of the 9.98789 here. Things are so bad, I'd kill for a follow-up gap. Now the question: What should I do?

Gushing With Gibberish in Jackson

A: Dear Gushing,
    LTTEAGBTM.[1]

Q: The girls in my quilting group and I are becoming increasingly dissatisfied with the hymn selection under our new church growth pastor. It seems (at least he says so) that research indicates that the little kiddies' ditties they play on the local Christian radio station are what people want to sing. The gals and I think it's mildly incongruous and profoundly infantile to wave our arms and wiggle our fingers while singing hymns. Have you ever seen seventy-five-year-old women getting into the "Arky, Arky" song? What should we do?
Distraught in Dubuque

A: Dear Distraught,
    Either learn the songs or transfer.

Q: The first thing our new pastor did when he arrived two months ago was to change our church motto to "The Church That Meets Felt Needs." The second thing he did was to pull out all of the pews in the sanctuary and install about 150 pool tables. Is this guy for real, or what?
Chalking It Up in River City

A: Dear Chalking It Up,
    Pool! With a capital *P* that rhymes with *T,* and that stands for ... *transfer.* Get out of there before he starts making you wear visors and arm bands on Sunday morning.

Q: We are a church that prides itself on its growth. Our DGR is off the board. But recently our pastor moved on, and the guy assigned to us is into liturgy, lots of formal language, confession of sins, creeds, and hymns like "We All Believe in One True God" (Long Version), "Isaiah, Mighty Seer in Days of Old," and "Guide Me, O Thou Great Jehovah." Our growth is still off the board, of course—but it's heading the other way. What should we do? Transfer?
Troubled in Texahoma

---

1. Learn to talk English and get back to me.

A: Dear Troubled,

Don't you dare! In that sort of situation you must work from within to change your pastor to get into a more growth-oriented worship service. Here are some tactics that have worked in the past: playing Christian rock music over the carillon system, stealing his sermon notes and making him go extempore, drawing big happy-faces on the back of his robes, and running around the parking lot during Sunday service and turning on the headlights of pioneers' cars.

Q: I've got this movie idea, okay? One night a blue-black glob of viscous muck lands in the education wing of a little suburban church. It's meeting night, right? And the only guy left in the whole place is an old negativist who is supposed to lock up before he goes home. Anyhow, there's something weird about this glob. The old guy pokes at it, right? And what happens but the next morning the guy is missing and the church has grown a new Sunday school classroom. Next week meeting night rolls around; half a dozen impossibility thinkers are sitting around after hours whining about this and that; the glob strikes again and—boom!—the place has a new sanctuary with Chartres-like stained glass windows and flying buttresses the next morning. What do you think? Pretty good movie concept, eh?

Cinematically Sanctified in Hollywood

A: Dear Cinematically Sanctified,

Not a good movie concept. A *great* movie concept. I've got a title for you: *It Came from Pasadena.* Or how about *The Blob with Church Growth Eyes?* Get back to me. I want a credit line.

Q: I'm a pastor assigned to a small rural church in North Dakota. It has never grown, and unless the lignite business takes off, it probably never will. I read that pastors will be evaluated on Judgment Day by the *results* of their efforts in evangelism and church growth, not by their efforts alone and, frankly, I'm worried. What should I do?

Miffed in Minot

A: Dear Miffed,

Pray that God delay Judgment Day or get transferred.

Q: If the most effective way to church growth is taking the gospel to the masses instead of the classes, and the emphasis is on reaching the less educated and lower socioeconomic strata of society, why are most of the megachurches extolled in church growth literature set in the suburbs and made up of upper-crust savants?

Looking for Answers in Lincoln

A: Dear Looking,
   Good question.

Q: My pastor is sensitive to the homogeneous unit principle. As a test he periodically says from the pulpit, just prior to the sermon, "There's a white Mercedes in the parking lot with its lights on," and then he doesn't give a license number. Two years ago, 68 percent of the men in attendance got up to check. But last Christmas only 50 percent left, and in June it was down to 27 percent. Are we in trouble homogeneity-wise?

Puzzled in Palos Verdes

A: Dear Puzzled
   There's too much fog for me to answer your question properly. I need more stats, more data. For example, how many of your people drive *black* Mercedes? Or BMWs? And if they don't drive Benzes or Beemers, how many have cellular phones or car TVs? A Volvo with a cellular phone and TV is equal to a white Mercedes as far as homogeneity goes. Also, Lincoln Continentals with fish symbol bumper stickers—you have to consider those, too. Send me the data and I'll give you a more complete answer.

Q: I'm a pastor who has just moved to a predominantly German town in Wisconsin. I want to use church growth principles and develop a type of evangelism and worship that is comfortable to their heritage. In short, I want to adapt to their culture and meet their felt needs. Unfortunately, half this town is Lutheran, the other half is Catholic. They *like* their liturgy and their old stodgy services. Should I adapt to the prevalent culture?

Bewildered in Burgherville

A: Dear Bewildered,
   Not if you want to grow.

Q: I have heard it said that church growth is really oriented to Reformed and Arminian theology. There's the disparagement of liturgy, the conspicuous silence on sacramental theology, and a doctrine of evangelism that presumes an Arminian view of conversion— the idea that converts participate in their conversion (thus the emphasis on experience that plays itself out in testimonials and sanctification-oriented sermons). Original sin also seems to be reduced to original weakness, hence an emphasis on perfection. Is this true?
                                        Wanting Some Answers in Atlanta

A: Dear Wanting Some Answers,
   Yes, but not officially.

Q: If spiritual-gifts inventories are such a revolutionary concept for mobilizing the laity, how come nobody ever thought of them before?
                                        Percontatorial in Pittsburgh

A: Dear Percontatorial,
   Because church growth wasn't invented until 1955.

Q: Recently I heard the pastor at a rapidly growing church excoriate "church shopping." He called on his people to develop a sense of loyalty. And yet he does everything in his power to attract people to his church. Glitzy services, celebrity testimonials, traffic cops all over the place, more programs than Health and Human Services. Isn't this, in effect, "sheep stealing" and a contradiction to his call for loyalty?
                                        Discombobulated near Disneyland

A: Dear Discombobulated,
   Call it "sheep finding" and you'll be okay.

Q: I am a liturgical pastor who holds a sacramental view of the Lord's Supper. Thus it is not open for all takers on Sunday mornings. Communicants must believe in the Real Presence and they must be members of my denomination before I allow them to come. I do this for their own spiritual welfare. This presents a problem in the matter of making visitors feel welcome. Visitors come into my church and then are *excluded* from the major part of the service. They just have to sit there and watch. What should I do?

Sacramental in Sheboygan

A: Dear Sacramental,

Don't have Communion.

Q: My people come in at a minus-five on the Distribution of Receptivity Scale. A left-end people if I ever saw one. There are many barriers to Christianity here—social, linguistic, and class. And they have come up with a strange religion. When I arrived, they were worshiping a broken satellite dish on the outskirts of the village. Shortly thereafter, a technically inclined missionary who was passing through got the thing to work. He tuned it to TBN twenty-four hours a day. Now, the villagers have begun to worship Jan Crouch—whom they call "She Whose Face Is a River"—although none of them understands a word she says. In seven years here, I have not made a single convert, and I'm sick and tired of it. I'm all for holding the resistance lightly and everything, but this is ridiculous. I want to be where the action is. What should I do?

Getting No Numbers in Deepest Darkest Latfricasia

A: Dear Getting No Numbers,

Get transferred.

Frank Talk from Pastor Frank (Tawke): "We Are Going Church Growth!"

Well, as I reckon you all know by now, I'm back. *I* sure know it. I am plumb wore out from answering that telephone. Good golly, folks! A fellow changes one or two picayunish things around this place, and you folks act like he is leading you into the depths of perdition itself. You folks have got your tongues put out everwhich-aways, and unfortunately, much of what you all are saying is plumb wrong. It is. That's why I'm sending out this special edition of "Frank Talk from Pastor Frank (Tawke)"—to get shed of some of the misunderstandings, and to allow a body to get a few winks of shut-eye around this place at night without the phone jangling in my ear.

But first things first. Let me say this: There ain't no preacher anywhere south of the state line what's been treated better than I have by you folks here at First Faithview. No, that's right. I mean it! I'm beholden to you all a gracious plenty. To let a fellow wander off for three months to find hisself and sort out things in his life and ministry—that takes a whole heap of loving on your part, and I thank you for it. I do. It did me a world of good, I guarantee that.

And now, I'm back! And I reckon I got it all figured out now—for me, for you, and for First Faithview, too. I done got all our problems licked, friends. We are going church growth!

Did you know that we are bad off here at First Faithview? We have had 185 members now for the past thirty-seven years—thirty-four of them under Pastor Delbert, and now three under me. As they say in Pasadeny, Californy—that's where I been to the past three months—we have "plateaued." Now, I don't know whether you know it or not, but it's give up to be that plateauing is bad. Real bad! In fact, it's so bad, we are diseased. When you don't grow, you're sick. And we are a sick bunch here at First Faithview—thirty-seven years worth of sick.

We are standing in the need of a cure, folks. And good old Frank Tawke has done got for hisself the one thing what's going to get old First Faithview back on its feet again. He has gone and got hisself a "vision for the future." The boys in Pasadeny give it to me. Yessir! And when I point my new "vision for the future" at First Faithview, know what I see? I see superchurch! I see megachurch! I see a big old sanctuary with padded theater seats in it that is just filled to overbusting every Sunday. I see choirs and orchestras and heaps and heaps of good old souls sitting out there gobbling up the gospel. I see good old Pastor Frank right up there in front, stalking that stage in a store-bought suit, flapping his Bible, and preaching his country heart out. That's what I see, friends. That's the vision the Lord done laid on me. I see three thousand members by 1993; five thousand by 1994; establishing Frank Tawke Ministries, Inc., by 1995; and by 1996, right here on the First Faithview grounds, Frank Tawke University! Oh, it *is* exciting!

But to make that vision into reality we are going to have to pay a mighty big price here at First Faithview—both you and me, too. We are going to have to do something that's awful tough to do. We are going to have to change.

And, as you all no doubt know by now, I already have begun to hold up my part of the deal. Been by the church lately? Seen anything different on the sign out front? Well, I did a little switching. Instead of "First Faithview" in those big old two-foot-high letters up the top of the sign, you will notice that I replaced them with my own name, "Frank Tawke, Pastor," and put "First Faithview" down the bottom in teeny-weeny letters. You prob'ly also noticed how big my name is up the top of this letterhead, and that my picture is up there too. And if you are very observant, you liked to have seen the big billboard on Main and Fourth, and the bus benches all along Third Avenue, and the full-page spread in the *Gazette-Times* and even the advertisement on the sides of the city buses. And you may have noticed that they all have one thing in common—my face and my name are on them.

You see, all the studies show that when outsiders come to a church, the one thing that influences them most is the preacher. He is the leader. He is the one they come fixing to hear and desiring to see.

And because I so desperately want First Faithview to become a mighty witness for the Lord in this community, I have allowed this type of advertising to happen, even though it is a high price for me to pay. You see, I am actually a very humble man, and seeing my name and face big as life all around town is tough on me. Do you think I like seeing my name so big on the sign? Do you think I enjoy seeing my face riding down the road on the side of some bus? Of course I don't. (And neither does Eula. She'd like to have died when she seen how they mommocked up the coloring on my nose wart.) I hate it! I do. But it is the high price I must personally pay to be a great leader and to lead First Faithview into great growth, and I am willing to sacrifice my own desires for unbiblical humility to do it.

Also, as we grow we will be hiring on a whole mess of new staff to help me out—assistant pastors and education directors and counseling-service folks and so forth. But no matter how big we get and how many assistants we have, I'll still be the one preaching every Sunday, week in and week out. That is one of the prices, too—a price I have to pay, not you (ha!). Think how unfair it would be to this city to see my name and face plastered all over town and then for outsiders to show up at church and some unknown third-rate storyteller is preaching when they were all fixing to hear the dynamic Frank Tawke? Why, they'd feel cheated something terrible. If there's one thing I learned in Californy, it is that church growth preachers are very high-profile fellows. Yes siree! In the spotlight, pushing all the buttons, preaching all the time—it's a price we got to pay.

But the biggest price I'm going to have to pay has to do with my role here at First Faithview. You know how I used to be before I left?

Good old Pastor Frank, the kind, gentle soul that knew everybody's name and everybody's relatives' names even, and visited everybody's house three times a year, and came on over more times when somebody's digestion broke bad on the chili down at Eartha's Eats, and was *always* at the hospital it seemed, cheering folks up that needed cheering, and counseling with anybody and everybody that needed a word of comfort. Remember that Pastor Frank? Remember how it was always good old Pastor Frank who you could count on when the burdens of life got too heavy? It was good old Pastor Frank who was always there to bail out your soul—not to mention your body (I still say that warn't Co-cola you were drinking that night, Buford).

Remember all that? Okay now, get shed of it! Because all that is the *old* Pastor Frank, Pastor Frank the Shepherd. Now I'm the *new* Pastor Frank, Pastor Frank the Rancher! Oh, I'll still be the same old Pastor Frank deep down, but now I won't have time to be worried about all those shepherding duties. I'm in the ranching business now, with lots of shepherds underneath me who will listen to all your problems. That'll free me up for dreaming dreams and thinking about possibilities. I ain't no down-home country parson nomore. I am a church growth preacher now, and church growth preachers need to be free for thinking BIG, for planning seminars and writing books and inspiring people to grow. I can't be bogged down with all kinds of shepherd duties.

And now, finally, I'm going to talk about you, and the prices you are going to have to pay for First Faithview to grow. First, I learned that if a church is going to be led into bigness by a powerful leader, there have got to be people who are willing to follow him. Leaders cannot lead if followers do not follow. And that's why I fired all the boards and committees the minute I got back. *That's* why there weren't no committee meetings Tuesday night, folks. Because there ain't no committees anymore! (At least not until I can get some new blood in this church.)

Now, now, don't go ripping up your offering envelopes just yet. Let me explain. It's not that you haven't been good followers in the past. With the exception of a few of you old coots, you have been terrific, good-hearted folks, and I 'preciate that in you and I love you for it. I do. But the fact of the matter is that you are pioneers—as they say in Californy. You've been here so long, and you've been sitting on those same committees so long, and moving from this committee to that committee and from this office to that office that you wouldn't know possibility thinking and church growth conscience if it came up and belted you one right in the chops. In fact, *you* are diseased, too. That's right. You're just et up with koinonitis.

You see, your problem is that you like each other too much. You've been through lots of trials and tribulations over the years and you've developed close personal ties with each other, and whether you know it or not, that's bad. Bad for church growth, anyhow. And as we march toward bigness, you will become my enemies here because you stubborn old sodbusters simply will not change. You ain't changed in thirty-seven years and you ain't about to change now. I guarantee it. And in church growth churches it's always the homesteaders versus the pioneers, it's always the new folks against the old codgers, and if a church wants to grow, the new folks have got to win.

That's why I fired you all from the committees—to make room for the homesteaders. I would have fired you all right out of the church totally—saved us a big pioneer-homesteader shootout down the road apiece—but then I'd be subject to get in hock with some denominational pooh-bahs somewhere, so I chickened out.

But I can at least close this special edition of "Frank Talk" with a word of counsel. First, I know some of you are going to say the price is too great to pay. You're going to tell me that you want First Faithview to stay the one big happy family it's been for the past thirty-seven years. And you're going to say, we want good old Pastor Frank the Shepherd back. We want him to get his face off all those billboards and bus benches and to come back and visit us and counsel us and pastor us like pastors are supposed to do.

Well, I promised you that word of counsel and I'm going to give it to you now. If you feel that way—transfer. Because I am Pastor Frank the Rancher now, and First Faithview is going church growth, and we all will be a whole lot happier if you do.

———

The Pastor Bob Chronicles:

Stories from the Field

Bob Gets Relevant

—Bob, are you all right?

—Hmm?

—It's not like you to stare at the TV like that, especially when it's not turned on.

—Yeah . . . well . . .

—And that's your fourth glass of wine since lunch.

—Oh, that? First Timothy five-twenty-three.

—A stomachache? No, Bob, there's something wrong. You're letting your work get to you again, aren't you?

—After this morning, wouldn't you?

—Good point.

—I can't help but see my quest for relevance in worship—to bring new meaning to all parts of the service—as an abysmal failure, dear. I'm just afraid my efforts to touch each and every heart in that sanctuary just did not come off this morning.

—Well, you did touch Gordon Crandall.

—So I gathered.

—You missed his heart, though, by roughly a foot. Good thing, too.

—What's the latest from the hospital?

—Thirty-two stitches. Nine inches farther to the right and you would be bringing new meaning to the art of the funeral eulogy come Wednesday or Thursday. . . . Why didn't you use a Frisbee?

—A Frisbee is so . . . uh . . . undignified. . . . Up until then it was going all right, though, don't you think?

—Well, it was exciting, I'll say that much.

—The mime troupe's rendition of the Apostles' Creed was quite meaningful, I thought. And using the youth drama group for the New Testament lesson was, if I do say so myself, a stroke of genius, although if I had to do it over again, I would put some restraints on their expression when they played the swine plunging into the sea.

—The oinking *was* disconcerting, dear.

—But the dance group portraying the Old Testament lesson— Joel, chapter one—that was the *coup de grace,* in my humble opinion.

—Is that right?

—And I don't care what you say, they *did* look like locusts.

—I know bumblebees when I see them, dear. . . . The identity of some of those costumed people that marched across the chancel was a little vague, though. Who were those people?

—The sermon illustration? Paraguayan gauchos, Cossack dancers, Andean milkmaids, Balinese finger mimers, Tibetan herdsmen, Djibouti tribesmen, and aboriginal hunters? It was plain to me what they were.

—You're right, dear. Throwing a Frisbee and having it sail around the congregation and come back to you in the pulpit to emphasize the unity of the global community would have lacked the requisite integrity.

—It had to be a boomerang. I just happened to miss.

—I'll say this much for you, though. You were a bastion of composure when Crandall went down.

—Well, I did shake a little bit when the paramedics came sprinting up the aisle. I only hope the message came through.

—Oh, something came through, all right. You should have heard it after the service.

—Tongues were wagging, were they?

—I haven't heard the narthex buzz like that since you brought new meaning to the Christmas Eve candlelight service by wearing fluorescent hot pink robes. . . . It's really too bad.

—I'll say it is. During the week I was picking hymnals off the balcony railing. I had that boomerang singing a tune.

—Um, that's not exactly what I had in mind.

—These people were born to gripe. Gripe, gripe, gripe. That's all I hear. I bring the gospel to them in innovative ways; I make every worship service a gala experience; and all I hear is moaning and groaning.

—Why don't you hit them with something different?

—Be reasonable, honey. Everything I do is different.

—That's what I mean.

—Surely, you can't mean . . .

—Why not? They haven't heard it in the four years you've been here.

—That old, dry-as-bones liturgy? C'mon, honey, get real.

—No, you c'mon. Get relevant.

Bob Goes Homogeneous

—Well, Bob, you're at it again, I see.

—Hmph . . . Wha-a-a?

—Here it is, Sunday afternoon, and once again you're throwing those things back like tomorrow the state goes dry.

—Back off, honey. I'm Lutheran.

—Not according to the sign, you aren't. You took it *off* the sign.

—Like liturgy, vestments, raised chancels, clergy-dominated worship, sacramental hocus-pocus, and hymns that are tough to sing, a denominational affiliation is just another obstacle to growth, dear. A barrier. And besides, half the people in the world can't even spell it right.

—Honey, I'm worried.

—*You're* worried? This is the last can of this stuff we have in the house.

—No, I mean about you . . . us . . . this . . . this situation here. The attendance. The offerings. We had forty in church today, all three services. Forty!

—Backdoor loss will do that to a church. We've hit a temporary plateau, that's all.

—Plateau?

—Well, okay. Minor negative growth, then.

—An annual growth rate of minus 1,347 percent is minor? . . . I told you a long time ago your outreach here was way too narrow.

—I was just attempting to meet the felt needs of a certain sector of the community.

—But you went too far. You cut too fine.

—The homogeneous unit principle is tried and true church growth doctrine, honey. Race, education, employment, language, culture, class, nationality—like goes to like.

—So you decide to gear your ministry to upper-level corporate management.

—Do you deny that those people have spiritual needs, too? Especially the way the market is rollercoasting these days. With the monied aristocracy of this city on continual tenterhooks, this is a very fertile field.

—Maybe so, but your approach, dear. Your approach is so . . . uh . . . well . . .

—My approach is vintage church growth—right out of the books. I blow in when the people are experiencing duress, say, after a week when the market falls a couple hundred points. I meet their felt needs. We have a big-time group conversion, a people movement, and—boom!—I've got an instant megachurch!

—Of millionaires.

—Right!

—But leather swivel chairs instead of pews? A tickertape hymn-board? A phone at every seat?

—Meeting needs, dear.

—Lay renewal weekends in San Moritz? A wintertime satellite church in Palm Springs? And your revolutionary Sunday school recruitment program? Ah yes, rounding up these kids in style.

—Now don't get sarcastic. Limosine evangelism is at the cutting edge of church growth theory, dear.

—And I'm not even mentioning the, ahem, *sermons,* dear. "Would Jesus Be a Program Trader?" "Ananias, Sapphira, and the Tithe: Practical Lessons for Today's World." "The Hostile Take-over—Doing It with *Agape.*"

—I subscribed only to the well-proven principle that every person should be able to become a Christian with that person's own kind of people. That's basic McGavran.

—That's all nice and everything, honey, but I see one problem with it.

—What's that?

—It's not working. Next Sunday I'm discontinuing the between-services buffet.

—Don't be hasty, now. We get one CEO who tithes and we're sitting pretty again.

—I say we go back to basics.

—But we expanded the parking lot *last* year.

—I don't mean those kind of basics, dear. I mean *basic* basics.

—What? And not give the people what they want?

—Right! Give them what they need.

Bob Has the Power

—Bob! Honey! Here you are . . . in the attic.

—Oh, hi, dear.

—What gives? Usually you spend Sunday afternoons drowning the morning's faux pas in rivers of brew.

—Not any more, dear. Don't need the stuff. "Be ye not filled with wine," and all that. I'm into headier stuff now.

—Oh?

—Yes. I'm up here awaiting personal revelation—a voice, a vision. I'd even settle for a dream, although I'm too wired to sleep.

—If I had stuck *my* hand into a basketful of rattlers, I'd be wired, too. I'm just thankful nobody brought any poison.

—Yes, that was a blessing.

—But why, honey? Why?

—Well, dear, research shows that charismatic churches are busting down the walls with growth. They're growing something fierce. And after my attempts with relevance and homogeneity, I figured this was the ticket. . . . However, I am a little worried about some of this stuff. Take the dancing in the Spirit this morning.

—Well, the children did seem to like the footprints you taped onto the floor.

—And considering the expense and effort I went to in establishing a separate, designated, safe "slain in the Spirit" area . . .

—Those were those tumbling mats spread out against the east wall?

—Right. . . . Nobody went down with the power all morning, unless you want to count the alleged "slay-ee," Herbert Glosscoat.

—And you were on him in a flash, waving your Bible and screaming. What was that all about?

—Honey, Herbert Glosscoat was sleeping! I was delivering him from the demon of lethargy.

—Oh.

—Now, I'm willing to admit that I do have a few things to learn, logistically. Like my sermon. You know, dear, for the first time in my ministry I got the impression some of the congregation were actually laughing at me during my sermon.

—Your sermon, dear?

—You know, when I ministered under the anointing and witnessed to a few of the things the Lord had laid on my heart.

—Too bad he didn't lay a few words on your lips, too.

—You noticed the pauses?

—Oh, I noticed the pauses! What I didn't notice was a sermon.

—The true charismatic preacher is wholly under the power of the Spirit, dear.

—So that accounts for the way you stood there for a seeming eternity before you threw your hands straight into the air, let loose with that weird and unintelligible martial arts kind of scream, and then went into that crazy . . . *thing* . . . down the aisle?

—A series of spasmodic gestures undertaken while under the power of the anointing is called the "holy jerk," dear.

—Looked more like the "holy watusi" to me.

—No. I'm almost sure it's the "holy jerk," dear.

—I see. . . . And now you're up here awaiting a new word from the Lord, eh?

—Right. Something. Anything.

—Well, I've received a word from the Lord myself, and that word is that we should not bind the power of the Spirit.

—Right on! That's what I've been saying all along.

—And that word is that we should emphasize the miraculous signs and wonders of God, as set forth in his Word.

—Oh, this is great! My prayers are being answered.

—And that word is . . . *sola Scriptura.*

—Don't hold back, dear. Let the Spirit go!

—*Sola Scriptura . . . sola fide, sola gratia, sola Scriptura.*

—Glow-ree! Honey, it's happened! The Second Blessing!

—No, dear. I mean the Bible, the Word alone that shows us the way to grace through faith and the signs and wonders of the Gospel and baptism and the Lord's Supper. If we neglect these miracles, we are binding the power of the Spirit.

—Aw, honey, I thought you had something exciting there.

Bob Learns the How-Tos

—A touch of the bubbly, dear?

—Champagne? What happened, Bob? Somebody say something nice in the handshake line?

—Somebody? Try everybody! I've had a "Eureka!" experience, honey. I have found what the people want!

—I hope you're not talking about that pabulum you dished out during this morning's sermon.

—Pabulum? A basic how-to sermon, pabulum? People are looking for God, dear. They want to know if God is real or not. They want to know where to find him. And the place I'm telling them to look is in the renewed life—in the quest for personal holiness.

—Look in your heart—there you shall find God, eh?

—Exactly.

—All they'll have then is faith in their faith.

—You're missing the concept, dear. Look, ours is a troubled world. Uncertainties at every turn. AIDS, drugs, sex, abortion, nuclear war, poverty, homelessness. Where is God in all of this?

—Anyone looking for God in the world is going to find wrath.

—Right. That's why we go to the heart. Feeling Jesus in your heart, turning this or that area of your life over to him, conquering a pet sin, using your spiritual gifts. I mean, these are things people can latch onto. They can see God's reality in their experience.

—Ergo, the how-to sermons.

—All based, I might add, on biblical principles. All using the Bible as a guide to show us the way to reach our full spiritual potential. I give them something they can take home and apply to their daily lives.

—And presumably, something they can come back to get more of the next week.

—You've got it, honey. You will notice my preaching schedule for the rest of the year.

—I've got it here. A series on the Beatitudes.

—You mean the "Be Happy" Attitudes.

—Okay. Then there's a series on the seven cardinal virtues, a series on Christian nutrition, and various and sundry series on Christian leisure, Christian exercise, Christian work habits, Christian money management, Christian entrepreneurship, Christian singleness, and—what's this?—Christian sex?

—I especially want you to be in attendance for that Sunday, dear.

—In addition to which, you will be speaking for eighteen consecutive Sundays on the book of James?

—And twelve Sundays on the book of Proverbs. Don't forget that.

—You're making the gospel into law, you realize that, don't you?

—Funny you should mention law. I've also got a series planned entitled "The New Moses."

—Who's that? Chuck Swindoll?

—No, Jesus.

—But that's heresy!

—You're calling a lot of pretty big-name preachers heretics, dear. Preachers who use the Bible as the Christian guide to daily living, who look at the characters of the Old and New Testaments, deduce practical principles from how they reacted to the crises in their lives, and apply that to daily living.

—I thought the Bible told us about a wrathful God who hates the sinner as sinner but who is also a merciful God who loves the sinner in Christ; in fact, One who loves enough to send his Son to die for him.

—Sure, I know that. Everybody knows that. But you can't tell them that every week. A lot of good that does people who are confronted with the enormous problems of everyday living.

—But the law condemns. It shows them how unworthy they are. They walk out of the place feeling grody as all get-out.

—No, they don't. They walk out with practical teaching for their daily lives.

—At which they will fail.

—And after which they will come back for more of the same. No, this time I've found it. The renewed life. That's the ticket. The stuff that works!

—You realize, of course, that you're selling out on everything you've ever learned or stood for?

—So?

—You're repudiating the preaching of law and gospel, of the doctrinal emphasis of your homiletics, the catachesis of the pulpit.

—I'm into the catechesis of lifestyle now, dear.

—You'll no longer be preaching the theology of the cross. You'll no longer be leading your people to the foot of the cross to see their humility and worthlessness before lifting them up with the sweet, wonderful news of God's love in Christ.

—So? I'll be helping people. I'll be meeting their needs.

—I see. . . . And you'll also probably grow like gangbusters.

—Now, honey, you're starting to make sense.

—But, dear, is it worth it? That's what I want to know.

—Worth it? I get hundreds, even thousands more in church on Sundays, meeting needs, meeting the people where they are, and you're asking me if it's worth it?

—Yes. I guess I am.

—It's worth it all right. . . . *Prost,* dear!

—*Prost?*

—To growth! To what works!

The Church Growth Inferno

The Church
Growth Inferno

_____

It was true. The ominous warnings and strident alarums, the angry missives and the sobbing cries—all of them, transmitted across the miles and over the years, had been true. I knew it the moment I pulled into the parking lot: my former congregation, an erstwhile bastion of orthodoxy, had gone church growth.

A new pastor, a veritable one-man gang of possibility thinking—the Reverend Seymour Peeples, by name—had burst onto the scene to break the shackles of stasis and lead the people into the promised land of largeness. The power elite, my friends from the early days, had opposed him and in consequence had been issued an ultimatum to change their nongrowth thinking or pack up their memberships and be on their malcontented ways.

I had been apprised of the outrage. Phrases like "power play" and "church growth takeover" and "spiritual blackmail" were threaded through the correspondence. "One day on the elders, next day out the door." "They act as if a vote against changing the church name is a vote against the Great Commission." "Get with the flow or out you go." It was inflammatory prose such as this that marked the jeremiads of my uncle, August Silage, one of the malcontents.

Indeed, the reports seemed convincing. But when the church of twenty-seven years of one's life allegedly goes the church growth

_____

route, one feels compelled to check it out in person, and the place where one looks for immediate verification is the parking. Surplus parking is the quiddity of church growth, the plumb line against which allegiance is adjudged. And when I turned the final corner on my way to church that hot, muggy Sunday morning last July, past traffic cops and orange-vested parking attendants and onto the church campus itself, I saw a sight capable of sending even the most jaded church growth consultant into frissons of delight. I saw a high-rise parking structure, twelve stories' worth, jutting into the sky. This was a church that had unquestionably gone church growth.

However, in the greeter queue I noticed something that made me think perhaps it had gone one step further. As unbelievable as it might sound, I got the distinct impression that I was under some type of surveillance.

Entrance to the narthex was gained only by running a gauntlet of six greeters, gratuitous types who lined the church steps with their hands pumping and their teeth flashing. As I negotiated this line, I noticed a private conversation being carried on by the greeter on the end and a man in a light blue suit, who, while listening to the greeter's whispered words, was alternately staring at me and at a photograph he held cupped in his hand.

Hmm, I thought. *I had obviously gained somebody's notice. Do I look like an impossibility thinker? Can they tell I don't have "church growth eyes"?*

By the time I had reached the end of the line, the man in the blue had moved to the side, and the last greeter—unctuously—led me to a special sign-in book where I was to enter vital information for follow-up reference by the church. So he said. But I know how that game is played. They make me sign the book, then during the service they run the information up to the front, and when the visitor recognition segment of the service rolls around, they spot me out and embarrass the heck out of me. Not for me, thank you. I hate that stuff.

So I bolted for the restroom, where, from behind a crack in the door, I saw the greeter and the man with the picture gesticulating angrily toward each other. I slipped out with a pack of boys and slinked along the wall in the opposite direction, nestling eventually into an inconspicuous niche from which I established my own surveillance post, watching for both the suspicious-looking fellow and any members of the herd I had run with fifteen years before.

None of which, I might add, was anywhere around. Of the hundreds of worshipers transiting the narthex in the busy preservice moments, none—not my uncle, not any other of my old cronies—was present. So, thinking I would catch them after the service, I marched into the sanctuary to assume a pew end at midnave, left side, as is my wont, and to sit back in air-conditioned comfort and enjoy the show.

Because, show it was. No longer did a staid and allegedly spiritless liturgy shield the unchurched masses from the meaning of worship. This was celebration—church growth style. From the pre-sermon praise singing to the Dorcas Guild's innovative, nonverbal interpretation of the New Testament lesson; from the glittering offering of a sixty-voice choir (with orchestra) to a pastoral pulpit entrance amid a cloud of smoke that would make Caesar's Palace blanch with ostentation—every aspect of the service was designed to impress.

I could empathize with my friends—how they must just *squirm* with uneasiness from invocation to benediction Sunday after Sunday. And as the sermon began, I freed my eyes to roam the sanctuary, scouring the rows for my old-time friends. I looked up one side and down the other. I checked the bulletin for familiar names. I inquired about my former pastor—the Rev. Wilhelm Peese—of the fellow seated to my right, and I wrote down some names and showed them to the person seated in front of me, then to the person to her right, but no one had heard of any of them.

Weird! My friends had been institutions at this place. The elders, to a man, had been baptized right here. Correspondence I had received since the takeover had resounded with the stolid avowals of a besieged minority—replete with pledges to fight to the bitter end. I leaned over to make additional inquiry of the fellow to my right, and as I did so, I saw the suspicious-looking fellow from the narthex leaning out and looking suspiciously at me. Great! My friends had all vanished from the face of the earth, and I had some guy trailing me with cryptic photos. What was going on?

But then the cumulative effect of two long days and as many short nights on the road began to entangle me in its soporific web, and by the time Peeples had got past his opening round of putatively humorous personal anecdotes, I found myself battling a serious case of the nods.

It's a battle nobody ever wins and, following the utilization of every trick I had ever used during my arduous cross-country driving stints, I found myself abruptly snapping my head to, catching only a cliché here, an aphorism there, before drifting off again into the troubled respite endemic to *homileticus interruptus.*

Finally, out of desperation, I decided to close my eyes. It is easier to concentrate with my eyes closed—fewer distractions and an increased ability to focus and no visual interruptions and . . .

"No, I don't know August Silage!" It was the narthex. It was coffee time. I was proffering snapshots from the 1973 church picnic to a bystander who, following an initial show of affability, had turned gelid with the fifth photo.

"Okay, then," I said. "Ever seen this guy?"

"No!" he snapped, without looking.

"How about this lady, then? Front row, second from the left."

"No, not her either. Look," he said, wheeling to face me full-front and tapping his empty Styrofoam cup against my chest. "I don't know Marion Schwanke. I have never seen Rheinhart Hinkel-winkel or Gustav Hornschwoggle or anybody else. Now, if you don't mind . . . Oh, Jerry! Jerry!"

He threw his hand in the air and began pointing downward toward me. A man in a sky-blue tuxedo, one of many such greeter types roaming the narthex on postservice visitor patrol, began sliding through the fellowshiping throng.

I had already met Jerry. He had seen my pictures, and he didn't like them either. Nobody seemed to like them. Nobody seemed to know anybody from the early years. It was not only the actual corporeal presence of my friends that was absent, it was every memory of them as well.

I slid quickly down the wall, past growth graphs, building-fund thermometers and greeter-of-the-month displays, and finally slipped inside a door and trotted down a flight of steps, pausing on the bottom to regroup. I was in the basement, a labyrinthine maze of corridors and passageways with hidden offices and mystery rooms stuck into every corner. Downhearted, I kicked along the webwork, attempting to recapture any vestige of the past. I trudged past storerooms and offices; I poked my head into meeting rooms and janitors' closets, consumed in thought, until something that I never dreamed could occur in a structure I knew so well did indeed occur. I got lost. From one corridor to the next I meandered, and then back again, past janitors' closets I was certain I had previously passed, over ground I knew I had already traversed. I began to worry. First I find absolutely no trace of anyone, and then I get lost inside my own church. What was I? The butt of some ecclesio-Hitchcockian ruse?

As I wandered deeper and deeper into this Chinese puzzle I was inexplicably drawn toward one closed door from behind which I thought I heard faint anguished and tortured cries. I was about to throw open the door when suddenly I perceived a figure in backlighted silhouette approaching from the darkness.

"Canst thou be Virgil?" I said, struck by an unaccountable desire to recite Italian poetry.

"You got it, man," came the reply as the figure marched resolutely near, his path bringing him out of the shadows.

It *was* Virgil—Virgil Jungkunst, head usher during my tenure, a man of consummate religio-political acumen who had a history, unlike that of my other acquaintances, of accommodation, not confrontation. "Am I happy to see you!" I cried.

"What are you doing here?" he said, grabbing my elbow and pulling me against the wall.

I explained. My ardent desire to return, to renew acquaintances, to see Silage and that crew, had proved futile. I had sought to recapture memories by plumbing this chthonian abyss, had subsequently lost my way, and had been drawn by torturous cries to this very place where it had been my unexpected privilege to confront the familiar face and bearing of what now represented my sole tangible link with a portion of my life spanning infancy to my twenty-seventh birthday. "Let's go tip some cold ones," I said. "We've got a lot to catch up on."

He eyed me with the kind of suspicious expression ushers use when they look at thermostats, and then in rapid staccato, he reeled off my name, my parents' names, my year of confirmation, a recounting of the time it took me eight minutes to light one candle during my acolyte days, and the fact that I had captained the 10:45 A.M. ushering team for six years. It was an awesome mnemonic display.

"You remember me, then," I said.

"I remember everybody," he returned.

"Well, then, where are they all?"

"What do you mean?" he said, his eyes narrowing.

"Uncle August. Schnaubelt. Finkelnob. Zubergut. Everybody," I said. "The early service was packed and I didn't recognize a soul."

"Oh," he said, peering up and down the corridor. "They're all, uh, occupied at the moment."

"You mean they're here?" I said.

"You might say that."

"Well," I said, my voice filled with importunity. "Where?" Just then a horrific scream flooded the corridor. "What was that?" I said, looking at Virgil. He looked at me, and then I lunged for the doorknob.

Virgil violently rammed his shoulder into me and pinned me motionless against the door jamb, his face now inches from my own, his every muscle taut with tension. For an old guy, he was *strong*. "What was what?" he said evenly.

"Why . . . that scream!" I said. "What do you mean, 'What was . . .'"—another scream, more piercing, more anguished, cut me off. I threw Virgil aside. "I'm going in there!" I yelled, lunging anew.

"Wait!" he shrieked. I stopped. Additional hugger-mugger glances issued from the sides of his eyes, and then he said, "I'll show you." Keys were produced and, opening the door, he led me down a seemingly endless, dimly lit passageway that narrowed gradually as we descended, the walls turning from plaster to wood to stone. We descended some steps, and the air turned cool and a misty veneer formed on the walls. Virgil snatched a flambeaux from a stand and led us onward until, finally, our descent was halted by a door, which he swung open. Before us spread a cavernous hall, of a size to match any of the great rooms at Carlsbad. All about the perimeter men and women were pinioned to the floor or bolted against the walls in stockadelike apparatus. What seemed like dozens of men in sky-blue tuxedoes gamboled about, howling derisively and mocking the captives. Every once in a while a shriek was sent out, the intensity of which gave me gooseflesh.

"What chamber of horrors is this?" I cried, stupified at the scene.

Virgil cast me a sinister eye. "We have come to see your friends," he said. "Come."

"My friends?" I shrieked.

Virgil nodded to a couple of blue-clad men lounging near the door, big men with obsequious and smarmy smiles who trotted immediately to his side, received furtive instructions, and then moved to a position at my rear, apparently to guard against attempted flight on my part.

I looked desperately at Virgil. "What is going on?" I pleaded.

"This is the place where we keep those who have opposed the church growth movement," he said. "These are the people who repeatedly questioned growth-oriented programs, who saw not with church growth eyes, who lived not with church growth conscience. They stood for smallness and the status quo, and then after it was all over, they refused to transfer." He spread his arms in diabolical malediction. "Welcome," he said, "to the Church Growth Inferno. Every growing church should have one."

We walked to a small room, one of what seemed like hundreds encircling the perimeter of the hall. "You recognize this guy?" he asked tauntingly.

"Schnaubelt!" I screamed, pointing at a squirming man shackled in a prone position on thick, bright red carpeting. I wheeled on Virgil. "What's he doing here? He was a pillar of the church."

Virgil strolled unmoved toward the prostrate victim and reached out with the tip of his boot, touching the man's forehead. "Hubert," he said. The man's eyelids rose slowly. "How do you feel about red carpeting now?" The old man wiggled furiously. Virgil turned to me. "This guy voted down red all-purpose carpeting for the sanctuary, despite conclusive evidence that red carpeting contributes to the warming of the human heart"—then to Schnaubelt—"And you wanted mauve, didn't you, Hubert?" The man was thrashing wildly. "Very limited church growth vision. Very limited."

"B-but why?" I stammered, but before I could move to help Hubert Schnaubelt, the henchmen had latched onto my arms and led me away.

"This is the First Circle," Virgil declared, sweeping his arm toward the great expanse of torture chambers. "Upper Church Growth Hell, as it were. These are they who have committed sins of thinking small, who have consistently exhibited behavior that has been unamenable to growth.

"These here," Virgil continued as we moved to the next cell, a grotto that housed eight people, their faces frozen in pain, all tied and gagged in basketball nets and fastened to a pew that rotated rapidly in a circle much like a carnival ride, "voted down portable furnishings in the sanctuary that allow us to pull everything out and host a neighborhood basketball league on Sunday afternoon. It's great publicity for the church."

"So you torture them?" I said. A henchman gave me a warning nudge.

"Yes sir, those old negativists are getting what they deserve," Virgil said, oblivious to my concern. He led me out of the great room and into another corridor, and as we progressed down its dark way, again it narrowed until finally after much walking we found our journey halted by another door, behind which emanated a peculiar rushing, gurgling sound. Virgil flung wide the door, and an odious stench swept over us.

"This is the River of Impossibility," he said, "and these are impossibility thinkers." Out of the fast-running stream of thick, brownish red fetid liquid poked several heads, their features frozen into visages of anguish, with only their mouths active, out of which proceeded a monotonal chant of indeterminate origin, providing eerie and unreal accompaniment to the already eldritch scene. We embarked from the shore in a small boat, motoring within feet of the heads, and it was here that I could first distinguish the words of their litany, spoken tutti, without vocal inflection. They were chanting questions and what Virgil referred to as "nongrowth excuses." "Why?" they chanted. "How come? It costs too much. It can't be done. The voters' assembly will never approve it." They sang it again and again until it took on a poetic life of its own: "Why? How come?/It costs too much. It can't be done./The voters' assembly will never approve it./ Why? How come?/ It costs ..."

But the stench—it was overpowering. I breathed through my mouth until we reached the other bank and what Virgil called the Second Circle, the Circle of the Nonperformatory. "Confined in this circle are they who opposed worship as performance," Virgil explained. "These are dour and colorless people who wanted to retain worship as ritualistic monotony with the same versicles and same responses, week in and week out, and in church growth, that stuff just doesn't wash. These people here, for example"—we had been moving during Virgil's exordium up, out of the boat, onto the nether bank, and through another narrowing aperture, into another capacious expanse similar to that of the First Circle. We halted in front of a cell where a dozen or so people lay in various poses of contortion on the floor, all covering their ears with both hands, while the recorded voices, jacking up full throttle, of contemporary Christian musical artists boomed out in song from gigantic speakers implanted in the roof and walls—"These here didn't like praise singing and contemporary Christian music. Once in a while, when it looks like we might lose one of them, we put on an old familiar chorale just to revive them momentarily, but then it's right back to the lively contemporary tunes that appeal so much to the unbelieving world."

We moved to the next grotto, where a dozen or so captives were strapped into folding chairs, their faces in pain and their heads averted, comprising a listening audience for another of their number who stood behind a podium up front, reading haltingly.

"What is their sin?" I asked.

"They were against more active lay involvement in worship. They didn't like lay readers, lay communion assistants, lay anything."

"What's he reading?" I asked, nodding toward the man at the podium.

"Genealogies," Virgil said. "Genesis 10 and 36, 1 Chronicles 1 through 9, Ezra 2, Nehemiah 7, Matthew 1, Luke 3. Listen." I listened. It was like my first-grade "Bluebird Reading Group" all over again. "He butchers every other word. Drives them crazy."

We moved on past many cells, all occupied by old-timers who had opposed church growth doctrine and were now meted out condign punishment for their sins. There were those who were skeptical of spiritual-gifts inventories, others who had opposed skitlike sermons. We passed some who didn't like guitars during worship, others who refused to clap their hands in church, and many, many more, all of whom had rejected the notion that worship be conceived as performance, as an event geared to appeal to outsiders first.

Virgil inclined his head toward another door, behind which stood the Pathless Woods of Church Growth Aphorisms, a large stand of withered trees in which recalcitrant church growth opponents were left to wander without guidance and without chance of escape. Greeters encircled the wooded area, each with a long window-opening pole. Should one of the captives attempt escape, the greeter prodded him back toward the trees while simultaneously yelling one of the apothegmatic utterances peculiar to the movement: "We count people because people count," "Turn problems into opportunities," "Change minus signs into plus signs," "Big is beautiful," "I've got to believe it before I see it," and so forth.

We circumambulated the Pathless Woods, and while we were so engaged, Virgil explained the peculiar ignominy of those incarcerated in the third and final circle, toward which we now progressed. All those we had witnessed to this point were mere dilettantes compared with the vile beings housed in the third tier, Virgil said. For in the Third Circle were housed those with the temerity to take the movement on on theological grounds.

"Now, don't get me wrong," Virgil said as we transited an inter-circle passage nearly identical to that bridging circles one and two. "We are all for theology. I mean, it's great and everything. Important and necessary and all that. But really, let's face it, it can be a real hindrance to church growth. . . . Take the guy on the end"—we were staring at a group of people pilloried in variegating postures, each with punishment being applied by his attendant torturer-greeter.

"What's wrong with him?" I asked.

"Acute doctrinitis. If you can believe it, the guy *wants* sermons about doctrine."

"What about the others?" I asked. "What are they in for?"

"Well, the second guy offered the usual antigrowth arguments at a voters' assembly: remnant theology; a glorification of smallness; numbers are not important, faithfulness to the gospel is; be small and be holy; we need to get better before we get bigger; quality versus quantity. Basic stuff. He was always quoting Bible passages like, 'Where two or three are gathered together, there am I in the midst of them'—there's a scribal error in that passage, by the way."

"Oh?" I said.

"Should read, 'Where two or three *thousand* are gathered together.' A few zeros got lost in the transmission. . . . And the third guy, his favorite hymn was 'Oh, Little Flock, Fear Not the Foe'—not exactly a growth-oriented hymn."

"You locked him up for that?" I said. But Virgil only smiled.

We moved down the line until we came to a cell in which a man, his back to us, stood at the threshold of a door upon which he knocked and which, through a mechanical device, was being continually opened and then subsequently slammed in his face.

"What's going on here?" I asked.

"This," Virgil said, "is a Search Theologian."

The man turned to face us. "Uncle August!" I screamed. Virgil's myrmidons grabbed my arms.

"He refused to accept a 'friendship franchise' at the church, our innovative *oikos* evangelism strategy, a sort of spiritual Amway, where members develop networks of friends and then evangelize them."

"How phony!" I said. "I don't blame him."

"Instead, the guy knocks on doors inviting people to church."

"What zeal! What love for the Lord!"

"Except that knocking on doors, if it doesn't work, is not pleasing to the Lord. The Lord doesn't want effort; he wants results. He wants what works. Consecrated pragmatism—that's the watchword. If it works, it's good. . . . But now, there's one more cell I've got to show you. You'll get a kick out of this."

They pulled me down a circular path into the bowels of the inferno, past more cells, some filled with miscreants, some in readiness for future opponents of church growth, on past a door that said, "Greeters' Lounge"—from behind which came howls of laughter—to a cell where an unbreakable pane of glass had been installed and where guards were posted. Behind the glass barrier was seated an old man in a black cassock and white surplice, his features molded into a defiant visage. A large sign "Agent of Satan" hung above his head.

"Why that's Pastor Peese!" I shrieked. "An agent of Satan? That's crazy!"

"Yes, indeed," said Virgil. "Pastor Peese spoke vehemently against the church growth movement; even from retirement he charged up these negativists in the old guard. Anyone who is against church growth *ipso facto* wants churches to remain small; he who wants churches to remain small is against the Great Commission; and he who is against the Great Commission is an agent of Satan. Ergo, the sign."

"B-but he baptized me and instructed me and confirmed me and . . ."

"And unfortunately, he also had the impropriety to stand in the way of the will of God. This is a very negative man. He is against everything. Watch this! . . . Hey, Peese!" Virgil banged on the window with his fist. "You hate everything that's new and exciting, don't you?"

The old fellow sat nonplussed behind the safety glass, his arms folded, his lower lip protruding in defiance.

"You were against the high-rise parking structure. You were against the spiritual-gifts inventory and lay involvement in worship and against Sunday school songs during worship and innovative services and clapping in church. You're against *everything!* Tell me something that you're *for.*"

The old man lowered his eyebrows and glared at the window as he sat on the edge of his chair.

"Come on, tell me. Tell me something you're for, old man."

"I'm for the total depravity of man," Peese said, his voice resonating in prophetic histrionics. "I'm for sin being sin and grace being grace."

"That's another problem with the man," Virgil said. "He preaches about negative and controversial topics, like sin, and that's a definite church growth no-no. What else, old man?"

"And I'm for pure doctrine and objectively oriented hymns and nurturing the members of this church with good, solid sin-and-grace sermons instead of selling out for gospel reductionistic pap in its place, and I'm for . . ."

"And that's why you're down here," Virgil interrupted. "That will not fly in a church growth church. You and your kind are a bane to church growth everywhere. Shame on you, Pastor Peese. Woe to you, Pastor Peese."

Just then the greeter-torturers in attendance took up the chant. "Shame on you, Pastor Peese. Woe to you, Pastor Peese. Shame on you, Pastor Peese. . . ."

"Will you please pass the Peace? Won't you please pass the Peace?" A man was shaking my arm.

"Huh? Wha-a-a? Where am I?"

"Peace of the Lord," he said, gripping my hand firmly. There was a big smile on his face. It was the suspicious guy down the row. It was Jerry, too.

"Oh, uh, yeah." I said groggily. "Peace of the Lord."

"I'm August Silage, Jr.," he said, pulling a snapshot from his light blue coat. "Only way I knew you is a picture Dad gave me. I was a little kid when you were here."

"Oh," I said. "Uh-huh. Your dad okay? Safe and everything?"

"Yeah, sure. Terrific! Knocking on doors as much as ever."

"And Hubert Schnaubelt and Marian Schwanke?"

"Yes, sure! They're all fine. They all transferred a year or so ago. This church here decided to start a satellite church out in the country—for the people who didn't like the changes. Pastor Peese, too. Came out of retirement to lead them. It's really growing. All old conservative people from other church growth churches. Anyhow, Dad wanted me to be sure to catch you here today. None of them will come to church here. Big shindig at the house this afternoon. I've been looking for you all service. . . . But, uh, I'll talk to you later," he said, nodding toward the lectern where the Reverend Seymour Peeples was handing the dais over to the minister for visitors, an elderly, white-haired man who was clearing his throat into the microphone.

"Do we have any visitors today?" the man asked. It was Virgil Jungkunst. "Please raise your hand. We want to give you special attention today."

I kept my hand down. I had seen enough of Virgil's "special attention" for one day.

The Ultimate Church
is the first Zondervan book
typeset on a Macintosh computer
with a publishing program called FrameMaker.
The text is 10-point Stempel Garamond,
and the chapter headings are Clearface.
The supervisor of composition was Nancy Wilson.
The reproduction proofs were output by
CompuCraft, Grand Rapids, Michigan.
The book was printed by Color House Graphics,
Grand Rapids, Michigan.